W9-BVE-007

FORTY CARATS

Forty Carats

ADAPTED BY *Jay Allen*

FROM A PLAY BY *Barillet and Gredy*

RANDOM HOUSE · NEW YORK

FORTY CARATS *was first presented on December 6, 1968, by David Merrick at the Morosco Theatre in New York City with the following cast:*

(*In order of appearance*)

ANN STANLEY	Julie Harris
PETER LATHAM	Marco St. John
MRS. ADAMS	Iva Withers
MRS. MARGOLIN	Polly Rowles
BILLY BOYLAN	Murray Hamilton
EDDY EDWARDS	Franklin Cover
MAUD HAYES	Glenda Farrell
TRINA STANLEY	Gretchen Corbett
MRS. LATHAM	Nancy Marchand
MR. LATHAM	John Cecil Holm
PAT	Michael Nouri

Adapted by Jay Allen
From a play by Barillet and Gredy
Directed by Abe Burrows
Associate Producer Samuel Liff
Scenery designed by Will Steven Armstrong
Lighting by Martin Aronstein
Costumes by William McHone

Synopsis of Scenes

Act One

Act Two

Murray Hamilton as BILLY BOYLAN and Julie Harris as
ANN STANLEY

ACT ONE

Before the curtain rises, we hear a Greek folk melody. This continues as the curtain rises and for a bit under the opening action and dialogue.

The scene is the terrace of a little café in Greece. There are two crude wooden tables and some stools, sheltered against the burning sun by reed matting. In the background we see the Mediterranean and a Greek mountainside with some small white buildings on it. Upstage, leaning against one wall, there is a big, expensive, but dust-covered American motorcycle. We actually see only part of it; the front wheel is offstage.

Standing behind the table on the right is ANN STANLEY. *She is wearing a wilted linen dress, and sandals on her dusty feet. An overloaded native straw basket is beside her. A large straw hat is leaning against the basket. She is wiping her face and neck with a large handful of Kleenex. There are a lot of used tissues on the table in front of her. Also on the table is one shot glass.*

Speaking into a wall telephone near the doorway of the café up left is PETER LATHAM. *He is a very young man, wearing khakis, shirt and sandals.*

PETER (*Into the phone*)   Look, *gyneka etho!* Lady here. *Gyneka etho!*

ANN (*Interrupts*)   What? What does he *say?*

PETER (*Waving at her to be quiet*)   *Gyneka etho* . . . lady here . . . lady stranded!

3

ANN Lady hot . . . hot!
>(*She sits at the table, takes the Kleenex box from the basket, and puts it in her lap; takes out a folding fan, and begins to fan herself*)

PETER (*Into the phone*) *Amaxi!* . . . *Amaxi!* . . . Broken . . . Chevrolet *spasmenos* . . . Broken . . . What? . . . I don't understand . . . Pedi? . . . Oh, *pedi* . . . But . . . but . . . okay . . . okay . . . (*Discouraged*) *Efharisto.* Thanks.
>(*He hangs up, and comes over to her table, shaking his head*)

ANN (*Gets up, putting the fan in the basket*) What did they say? Will someone come?
>(*Music fades out*)

PETER No chance. The mechanic's having a baby and there's no doctor.

ANN (*Sits*) A baby! What am I going to do about my car! How am I going to get back to Argos?

PETER I've offered you a ride on my bike . . .

ANN And I've told you I couldn't possibly ride on that thing.

PETER Why not?

ANN I am thirty-six years old!

PETER Oh . . . Maybe if you tried side-saddle. (ANN *gives him a look*) Wait a minute. I know what you need. I'll be right back. (*He goes into the café. Out of the straw carryall* ANN *pulls a box of Baggies, tears one off, and starts to fill it with the used Kleenexes. In a moment,* PETER *comes out with a bottle and a glass, puts them on her table, and starts to pour.* ANN *puts a rubber band around the Baggie and re-*

4

places it neatly in her basket) This should help. As soon as you're finished with that Kleenex commercial.

ANN   You do make yourself at home.

PETER   I come to this little joint all the time. I've been camped down on the beach for a couple of weeks.

ANN   Doing what?

PETER   Painting.

ANN   Are you an artist?

PETER   No.

ANN   A student?

PETER   No.

ANN   What are you then?

PETER   What do *you* think I am?

ANN   I think you're a nutty kid, bumming around on a motorcycle.

PETER (*Amiably*)   That's what I am. A nutty kid bumming around on a motorcycle.

ANN (*Looks at the drink*)   What's this?

PETER   Ouzo. Try it.
     ANN *reaches into her straw bag, takes out her own drinking glass, and pours a drink from the glass on the table into her glass. Takes a sip, and looks pleased. Smiles at* PETER)

ANN   How old are you?

PETER   Twenty-two.

ANN   You don't look twenty-two.

PETER   You don't look thirty-six.

ANN I don't look thirty-six because I'm thirty-eight. (*Empties the glass*) I took two years off for good behavior. (*Pours another drink*) So just don't expect me to go roaring off cross-country on *that* thing. (*With no warning,* ANN's *face puckers up and big tears begin to course down her cheeks*) That . . . thing.

PETER (*Defensively, refers to the motorcycle*) That *thing* happens to be a Triumph Trophy Two-Fifty. (*Becomes aware of her tears*) Hey, don't . . .

ANN (*Puts down her drink, and rises*) What do you mean, hey, don't? I'm out here on a dead-end road with no traffic, a broken-down car, and a pregnant mechanic. And it's so hot! I go off and leave my mother with a *fantastically* upset stomach. She's had it for four days and she didn't want to come to Greece in the first place.

PETER You traveling with your mother?

ANN (*Defensively*) What's wrong with traveling with my mother? She's a charming woman and she's throwing up in that rotten little hotel. (*Sighs deeply*) Well, if I've got to spend the night here, I'd better see about getting a room.

PETER A room? *Here?*

ANN Well, a bed . . . in someone's house. (*He laughs*) What's so funny?

PETER (*Straightens his face*) Nothing. Bugs aren't very funny.

ANN *Bugs?* I shall sleep in the car.

PETER I'll lend you my sleeping bag. You'll be more comfortable.

ANN I'll be quite comfortable in the car.

6

PETER   No, you'll be quite miserable in the car.

ANN   Nevertheless. (*She picks up her bag*) How much do I owe you?

PETER   What for?

ANN   My share of the drinks.

PETER   Thirteen cents. (*He goes to her, and solemnly holds out his hand. She realizes he is teasing her; her lip begins to tremble again. She sits on a stool on the right*) Now don't start tearing up again . . . look—will you just relax and let me handle this situation? If you're determined to wait here until the mechanic shows —which will certainly not be until tomorrow—you might as well be comfortable. Wait at my place.

ANN   What's your place?

PETER   I told you I have a sleeping bag.

ANN   Sleeping bag?

PETER (*Points*)   Right down there.

ANN   Thank you, no.

PETER   Come on, hop on.

ANN   *No, thank you.*

PETER   You think I'm going to turn you back to mummy with "Hell's Angels" branded on your behind? Come on.

ANN   I am spending the night here . . . (ANN *turns furiously and marches toward the café door*) Vo-ee-thai astynomia, epharisto psomi, apototos . . .
    (PETER *listens to a moment of this, open-mouthed*)

PETER   What are you saying?

7

ANN (*Furious with frustration*) How do I know? I don't speak Greek. I want food! I'm hungry. I have a very fast metabolism.

PETER (*After a beat, goes to her*) Now look, it'll take me about fifteen minutes to spear a fish . . . a nice big fish. It's what I do for dinner every night. I'll build a fire on the beach and grill the fish with some fennel. I've got some tomatoes and onions . . . We can go for a swim, then eat.

ANN Swim. (*Turns to* PETER) I don't have a suit.

PETER (*Blandly*) Neither do I.
(*Greek music starts. She looks at him for a moment, crosses up to the table.* PETER *follows. She pours herself another drink, and sips it. We should begin to suspect that she is just a little high*)

ANN (*Trying to remember*) What did you call this drink?

PETER Ouzo.

ANN Ouzo! (*Drinks*) It certainly is! (*She looks around and sighs deeply*) Oh, it's all so beautiful here. What's that smell? It's so sweet.

PETER Myrtle. The whole island is covered with it. Myrtle is the flower sacred to Aphrodite.

ANN (*Vaguely, dreamily*) It is?

PETER And the bay down there . . . Yithien . . . that's where Paris first made love to Helen after he carried her off.

ANN Of *Troy* Helen?

PETER (*Turns, and points in another direction*) I think they're supposed to have spent a night over there, too

8

. . . it's the same legend all over Greece . . . Hey, before we go swimming . . . what's your name?

ANN (*A beat*) . . . Penelope.

PETER (*Extending his hand*) I'm Peter Latham.

ANN Peter Latham.
(*They shake hands*)

PETER And what I'm offering here is a cool dip in the blue Aegean, a gourmet meal, civilized conversation . . . in *English* . . . (*Smiles charmingly*) You'll forget your troubles.

ANN Will I?

PETER It's a promise. Come on.

ANN (*A beat*) Should I?

PETER Sure.

ANN (*Drinks*) Really?

PETER (*Gently, seriously*) Yes, I really think you should.

ANN (*Rises*) Should we bring the bottle?

PETER Great. Come on.
(*He picks up the bottle. She starts for the motorcycle, then stops*)

ANN Oh, dear . . .

PETER (*Goes to her*) What's the matter?

ANN I was just wondering how Helen of Troy managed about her mother.
(*There is a blackout. Then Greek music is heard*)

9

The scene is a real estate office in the East Sixties of New York City. There is a desk on the right, files upstage, a map of Manhattan on the left. A door to ANN's *private office is on the right; the entrance door and a bench are on the left. There is a chair in front of the desk. On the walls are plans of apartments, and photographs.*

Onstage is a woman, MRS. ADAMS, *very well dressed, looking over a list and shaking her head.*

MRS. ADAMS   No. . .no. . .no. . .
>   (MRS. MARGOLIN, *the office secretary, enters from the office door on the right. She is a motherly woman, sensible, good-natured, businesslike. She looks at* MRS. ADAMS, *then turns and speaks to* ANN, *who is not seen*)

MRS. MARGOLIN   Mrs. Adams is still here.

ANN (*Offstage*)   Please ask her to wait, Mrs. Margolin . . . I'll be with her in a few minutes.
>   (MRS. MARGOLIN *closes the door, and addresses* MRS. ADAMS)

MRS. MARGOLIN   Mrs. Stanley is still busy. She has a client in there.

MRS. ADAMS   I really *must* speak to her. There's nothing on this list. Nothing, nothing, nothing.

MRS. MARGOLIN   Mrs. Adams, that's the best list of apartments in New York.

MRS. ADAMS They're all impossible . . . No, here's one that doesn't sound too bad. Ten-eighty Park Avenue. What is the cross street?

MRS. MARGOLIN Eighty-eighth.

MRS. ADAMS Eighty-eighth. (*Disappointed*) It sounds perfect. But it's too far uptown—if you could give me this same apartment in the sixties . . .

MRS. MARGOLIN (*Gently*) We can't. It's attached to the building. (*The phone rings. She sits as she answers it*) Stanley Realty . . . Yes . . . which one? . . . Oh, yes, of course! That's a marvelous apartment. And a lovely building—beautifully run. There's a closed-circuit television guarding all the elevators, closed-circuit television at the front door and at the back, and there are one-way see-through holes on both front and service doors of every apartment. They've put in newly patented unpickable locks with chains, and it's a *lovely* neighborhood! (*Listens*) Well, that *is* what you pay for, isn't it? . . . Well, *we* think the price is very reasonable . . . One hundred and sixty thousand, plus a maintenance of . . . Hello? Hello? (*Hangs up, mutters*) That price is a real hangup.

> (*A man comes in, not handsome, but attractive and very sure of himself. He is smoking a cigar. He is* BILLY BOYLAN. *He seems quite at home as he goes to* MRS. MARGOLIN)

BILLY Hi, there, Mrs. Margolin!

MRS. MARGOLIN The actor's back.

BILLY (*Pinches her cheek*) The actor's back. Can I see Ann?

MRS. MARGOLIN She's busy now. You'll have to wait. You know, she just got back from Greece.

BILLY   How was Greece? Did she have a good time?

MRS. MARGOLIN   Well, she went with her mother . . .

BILLY   You have answered my question.
(*He goes to the bench on the left, sits, smiles politely at* MRS. ADAMS, *opens a magazine, and starts to read, puffing on his cigar.* MRS. ADAMS *watches* BILLY *covertly.* MRS. MARGOLIN *busies herself with papers*)

MRS. ADAMS (*Finally to* BILLY)   Don't I know you?

BILLY (*Pleasantly, but without any encouragement whatever*)   I don't think so.

MRS. ADAMS (*Persistent*)   Do you live in the neighborhood?

BILLY   No.

MRS. ADAMS (*Sits by* BILLY *on the bench*)   Are you sure we haven't met?

BILLY (*With a smile*)   I'd remember.
(*He returns to the magazine*)

MRS. ADAMS (*Takes this as a compliment*)   Oh . . . but I mean *really,* I could swear I've seen you . . .

BILLY (*Shrugs*)   Movies . . . television . . .

MRS. ADAMS (*Delighted*)   Oh, that's it! You're . . . you're . . .

BILLY (*Cutting in wearily*)   Billy Boylan.

MRS. ADAMS   Of course. You're *Billy Boylan.*

BILLY (*Nods*)   Billy Boylan.

MRS. ADAMS   Billy Boylan. (*She looks at him*) Are you

looking for an apartment? Mrs. Stanley has a lot of theatrical clients.

BILLY (*Rises*)   Yes, she has.

MRS. ADAMS   I'll bet she's a big fan of yours.

BILLY (*He can take no more*)   I doubt it. I used to be her
husband. Say, Margy . . .

MRS. ADAMS   Oh!
(*Ann comes out of the office, carrying some papers*)

ANN   Somebody left a blueprint out of this file.

MRS. MARGOLIN   *You* did.

ANN   Hello, Billy. You're back.
(*They embrace*)

BILLY   I'm back.

MRS. ADAMS (*Rises, and goes to* ANN *and* BILLY)   Oh, Mrs.
Stanley . . .

ANN   Oh, Mrs. Adams, I'm so sorry I've kept you waiting.

MRS. ADAMS   There's not a thing on this list that interests
me.

ANN   Oh, for goodness sake, Mrs. Adams . . . (*Takes the
list from* MRS. ADAMS, *and gives it to* MRS. MARGOLIN.
Sternly to MRS. MARGOLIN)   There's nothing on *that* list
for Mrs. Adams.

MRS. MARGOLIN   Of course not!

ANN (*Hands* MRS. ADAMS *her bag and gloves and begins to
usher her toward the door on the left*)   Mrs. Adams, if
you'll just give me a couple of days . . . well, make it next

month, I have something coming in that I know you'll love.

MRS. ADAMS (*Excited*)   What is it?

ANN (*Going ahead of her to the door, and opening it*)   I can't say anything about it now.

MRS. ADAMS   Mrs. Stanley, if you can't trust *me* . . .

ANN   I really can't talk about it yet. (*Whispers*) Big divorce coming up.
    (MRS. ADAMS *embraces* ANN)

MRS. ADAMS   Oh, a divorce apartment! They're always the best!
    (*She goes*)

ANN (*Calling*)   Watch the columns, Mrs. Adams. (*She closes the door on the thoroughly satisfied* MRS. ADAMS, *and goes to the desk*) She's a *looker*. Been *looking* through us for ten years. (*She takes a blueprint from* MRS. MARGOLIN) Have to see you later, Billy.

BILLY   Wait a minute. How was Greece?

ANN   Oh . . . (*A thought*) It was covered with myrtle.
    (*She goes*)

BILLY (*To* MRS. MARGOLIN)   Myrtle? Hey, Margy, the trip seems to have done her good. (*He sits in the chair in front of the desk*) What's she up to? Is she happy?

MRS. MARGOLIN   In her opinion, she's happy. In my opinion, she should have a husband.

BILLY   She's had two husbands.

MRS. MARGOLIN   Are we counting you?

BILLY   Certainly, we're counting me. She got a customer in there?

MRS. MARGOLIN   A rich one. Owns a string of hotels.

BILLY   Great. (*Pause*) How's business generally?

MRS. MARGOLIN   You can't be broke again.

BILLY   There's no such word as "can't"!

MRS. MARGOLIN   But you've had three shows in the last month. I read where you go from New York and L.A., L.A. and New York . . .

BILLY   I stop off in between.

MRS. MARGOLIN   Las Vegas.

BILLY   Where else? Newark? Margy, I'm a lonely, rootless man.

ANN (*Reenters quickly*)   Margy, can you get me the keys for Eight-Eighty?

MRS. MARGOLIN   Got him hungry?

ANN   Maybe.

BILLY   Annie! You're looking absolutely gorgeous. I've never seen you so goddam radiant!

ANN   You can't be broke again.

BILLY   I'm a lonely, rootless man. Just till the first, Annie.

MRS. MARGOLIN (*Hands* ANN *the keys*)   Here you go.

ANN   Thanks, Margy. (*Turns to go, then turns back to* BILLY, *waving the keys at him*) If I put this one over, I'll help you out. How much do you need?

BILLY   I need a thousand. (ANN *starts for the office door*) But I'll take five hundred.

ANN (*Turns back*)   Thanks. I need the money.
(*She goes*)

BILLY (*Starting for the door*)   'Bye, Margy.

MRS. MARGOLIN   Mr. Boylan, you're a lonely, rootless son of a bitch.

BILLY (*Turns back at the door*)   Don't, Margy, that's what my mother used to call me.
(*He goes. EDDY EDWARDS enters from ANN's office, followed by ANN. He is a big, well-set-up man in his forties*)

ANN   Mrs. Margolin, Mr. Edwards has decided he's quite interested in Eight-Eighty. I'm going to take him over for a look.

EDDY   You wait here while I go whistle up that driver. He had to park around the block. We'll be out front in three minutes.

MRS. MARGOLIN   Oh Lord, Eight-Eighty! (EDDY *stops and turns*) I promised the Bigelows we'd hold off for at least another week on Eight-Eighty until they know whether their daughter . . .

EDDY   You got another buyer for the place? (*Turns to ANN*) Look, Mrs. Stanley, you show me the layout, and if I like it you've got my check this afternoon.

ANN   I'll take it.

MRS. MARGOLIN   And I'll take care of the Bigelows.

EDDY   Thanks, Mrs. Margolin. I like your style. (*He starts off and turns again*) You and I are going to get on just fine. What do you drink?

MRS. MARGOLIN (*After a moment's thought*)   Diet Pepsi?

EDDY   You'll get a case.
(*He goes.* MRS. MARGOLIN *grins, and goes back to the desk*)

ANN (*Sits in the chair in front of the desk*)   I'm glad you reminded me about the Bigelows . . . *What* Bigelows! You made them up!

MRS. MARGOLIN   I lead a rich fantasy life.
(*She looks at* ANN's *shoes and frowns*)

ANN   What's wrong?

MRS. MARGOLIN   Why don't you ever wear those cute red pumps?

ANN   I hate them. They hurt.

MRS. MARGOLIN   He's a bachelor. Limp a little.

ANN   Mr. Edwards?

MRS. MARGOLIN   He's rich. He makes quick decisions. Limp a little.
(*She sits at the desk*)

ANN   Margy, will you get it through your head that I am no longer a Venus flytrap. I am thirty-eight years old—going on thirty-nine.

MRS. MARGOLIN (*Hands over ears*)   I didn't hear it! I refuse to hear it!

ANN   You heard it. For the thousandth time, I am a middle-aged woman with a seventeen-year-old daughter. (*She rises, and starts for the door. The phone rings*)

MRS. MARGOLIN (*Picks up the phone*)   Stanley Realty . . .

ANN   See you tomorrow, Margy.

MRS. MARGOLIN (*Into the phone*) Will you hold it a minute, please? (*To* ANN) You call thirty-eight middle-aged!

ANN Sure.

MRS. MARGOLIN I have never been so insulted in my life.

ANN Give up, Margy. We all gotta go sometime.
(*She goes*)

MRS. MARGOLIN (*Into the phone*) Sorry to keep you waiting . . . Yes, we handle suburban rentals. Could you give me some idea of the price you had in mind? . . . About a hundred and fifty a month . . . *Where?* . . . In Greenwich. Well, I really don't think you're going to find anything in Greenwich for that price . . . Well, look, dear, would you be willing to go a little further out of town? . . . Well, like Cleveland.

Blackout

SCENE THREE

The scene is the living room of ANN'*s apartment. It is almost six in the evening. Very loud rock music is heard over the radio. As the curtain rises* MAUD, ANN'*s mother, is sitting, legs outstretched, on the divan, reading a magazine. She wears a simple smart dress suitable to her age. But on her legs are bright red stockings, and she is wearing large pearl earrings.*

After a moment, TRINA, *her granddaughter, enters from the hall.*

TRINA (*Without looking at* MAUD)   Granny, have you seen my big pearl earrings?

MAUD   No, dear, I haven't. (*Searching for the earrings,* TRINA *moves first to the desk, then to the bar, and finally spots the earrings on* MAUD'*s ears.* TRINA *crosses, turns off the radio, goes over to* MAUD *and takes off the earrings*) Oh! I didn't realize I had them on.

   (TRINA, *having retrieved the earrings, has begun to sniff suspiciously*)

TRINA (*Behind the sofa*)   What's that? That perfume? (*Accusingly*) That's my *Jolie Madame.*

MAUD   I didn't realize I had that on.

TRINA   Granny, will you please stay the hell out of my *Jolie Madame?*

MAUD (*Quickly taking the offensive*)   Why do you wear your hair like that? It ruins your profile.

TRINA (*Suddenly looks at* MAUD'*s tights*)   Those tights. Those red tights!

MAUD What red tights?

TRINA (*Attempts to pull up* MAUD's *skirt.* MAUD *fights back*)
Those are my red tights, and don't tell me you didn't
realize you had them on.

MAUD Oh, I realized I had them on. I just didn't realize
they were red.

TRINA Look, Granny, I don't mess around in your Supp-
Hose.

MAUD Trina, what time did you come in last night?

TRINA (*Moving to the mirror and putting on the earrings*)
Around five.

MAUD Five A.M.?

TRINA Five A.M.

MAUD You haven't even the decency to lie. Who were you
out with till five A.M.?

TRINA Mark and Rudy and Bert.

MAUD Mark *who?* Rudy *who?* Bert *who?*

TRINA (*Turns back to* MAUD) Who goes formal? They're
just kids I go dancing with or shoot a little pool.

MAUD Shoot a little pool! How feminine!
(*The doorbell rings*)

TRINA (*Starts for the door*) It's Arthur for me.

MAUD (*Assumes a sitting position on the sofa*) Arthur?
You've never mentioned an Arthur. Arthur who?

TRINA I'll ask him when he comes in.
(TRINA *opens the door. We see the young man. He is*

the same one we met in the Prologue, PETER
LATHAM. *He is now wearing a white turtleneck
sweater and is carrying a sports jacket)*

PETER *(Confidently entering)* Hello. Are you Trina
Stanley?

TRINA Yes. Who are you?

MAUD He's *Arthur.*

PETER Peter.

MAUD Arthur Peter. All right.

PETER Didn't Arthur call? (TRINA *shakes her head)* Oh,
well, since he lives right around the block from my date
and I'm over here by you, we exchanged. *(Sees her blank
look)* I mean, I'm picking you up for Arthur and he's
bringing my date.

TRINA *(Accepts this. They start to go.* TRINA *opens the door)*
Okay.

MAUD *(Sharply)* Trina, if you don't mind. I'd like to meet
Arthur.

TRINA *(Closes the door, brings* PETER *into the room)* This
isn't Arthur. This is Peter. My grandmother, Mrs. Hayes.

MAUD How do you do? *(As they shake hands,* PETER *helps*
MAUD *to her feet)* Thank you. And where are you de-
livering my granddaughter this evening?

TRINA *(Impatiently, moving away)* 'Night, Granny Maud.

MAUD *(Following her)* But I wish to know where "Peter"
is taking you, Trina.

PETER We're going to meet Arthur and the others at the
Electric Circus.

MAUD (*Moves toward* TRINA) Then on to some pool emporium, I assume?

TRINA (*Her voice rising*) You'll pay for this, Granny!

MAUD I simply want to know where you're . . .

TRINA I'll tell you what, Granny, take off my tights. Right now! Take them right off!
(ANN *enters from the bedroom, wearing a robe and slippers and carrying a bottle of Vitabath and a towel*)

MAUD You are not leaving this house with a boy whose last name you don't even know!

ANN My Vitabath's all gone! Who's been . . .
(*She goes to* TRINA *and* MAUD. *Suddenly she stops, turns, as she realizes* PETER *is standing there*)

TRINA Granny did it.

MAUD (*Facing* TRINA) Ann, this young man, whom Trina has never met—nor, I gather, even heard of—rings the doorbell as a proxy for Arthur . . .

TRINA He had the decency to pick me up as a *favor* to Arthur!
(*Throughout the above exchange* ANN *casts stunned glances at* PETER. PETER, *at first surprised, quickly smiles his pleasure at seeing* ANN)

MAUD Arthur *who?*

TRINA How do *I* know! He's a friend of Peter's!

MAUD Peter *who?*

PETER Peter Latham.

TRINA (*Triumphantly*) Peter *Latham!*

MAUD   Peter Latham. All right! (*Thoughtfully*) Latham . . . I went to school with a Latham girl. From Pittsburgh. Isabella Latham.

PETER   She's my aunt.

MAUD (*Absolutely delighted, turns toward* PETER)   No! Isn't that extraordinary! If Isabella is your aunt, then you're a *Hohenhauser*. (*Suddenly all charm and social graces*) What a teeny-weeny world! (*She starts toward* PETER, *pushing* ANN *ahead of her*) Well! Ann dear, this is Peter Latham. This is Trina's mother, Mrs. Stanley.

ANN   How do you do?

PETER   How do you do, Mrs. Stanley?

MAUD   Trina, please ask Mr. Latham to sit down.

ANN   No! Mother, he doesn't want to sit down. Can't you see they want to go along? Have a nice evening, Trina. (*Kisses* TRINA, *pushes her toward the door. To* PETER) Don't . . . stay out too late. Good night . . . uh . . .

PETER (*Starting to go*)   Peter.

ANN   Good night, Peter.

MAUD (*Following* PETER)   Good night, children. Have fun.

PETER   Good night, Mrs. Stanley.

TRINA (*At the door with* PETER)   Good night, Mummy. Good night, Granny Maud . . . (*Shakes her head*) You really are something else! Come on, Pete.
      (*They exit*)

MAUD   A Hohenhauser! Ann, a *Hohenhauser!*
      (*Sits on the arm of the sofa*)

23

ANN (*Shakily begins to fix herself a drink at the bar*)　Tell me about the Hohenhausers. They're in steel, aren't they?

MAUD　Ann, dear, the Hohenhausers are in *money*.

ANN　And the . . . Lathams?
(*She slugs down the drink, then pours herself another*)

MAUD (*Eagerly*)　Well . . . Isabella Latham had I think it was two brothers. Or was it three? Oh well, *that* doesn't matter. What matters is that this one brother married the Hohenhauser girl who must have inherited *everything* . . . and this boy . . . this *Peter*, is the *son*. Didn't you think he was absolutely charming? How old do you think he is? About twenty?

ANN (*Slugs down another drink, then speaks quite definitely*)　Twenty-two.

(*There is a blackout. Then rock-'n'-roll music is heard*)

It is late afternoon, two days later, in ANN's *office.* MRS. MARGOLIN *is typing.* ANN *enters from her own office, and puts her purse on the file.*

ANN   It's after five. Why don't you go on home?

MRS. MARGOLIN   I'm just finishing up this lease . . . (*As she rises the phone rings. She picks it up*) Stanley Realty . . . Who's calling? (*Lifts her eyebrows, pleased*) Oh, Mr. Edwards. . . . Mrs. Stanley is right here. Just a moment.
　　　(*She hands the phone to* ANN)

ANN   Hello, Eddy, I was just about to leave . . . oh . . . well, dinner sounds fine . . . No, no, I'd really rather go home first and get myself pulled together . . . oh, give me about an hour and a half . . . Fine. See you then . . . Oh, it's apartment eight-B. "B" as in . . .

MRS. MARGOLIN   Bouillabaisse.

ANN   Bouillabaisse . . . Okay? . . . 'Bye.
　　　(*She hangs up. During the above,* MRS. MARGOLIN *has been standing near the desk, listening to the conversation with great interest*)

MRS. MARGOLIN   You must have limped real good.
　　　(*She goes to the coatrack and starts to get into her coat*)

ANN   I'm helping Mr. Edwards with the decorating. The basic colors.

MRS. MARGOLIN   Good. Keep the whole business basic.

ANN   Margy, I'm not interested in Mr. Edwards.
(*At this moment the outer door opens and* PETER
enters. ANN *freezes.* MRS. MARGOLIN *sees her
look, turns and sees* PETER. *He is very cool, very
in control*)

PETER   Hello, Mrs. Stanley, I'm glad I caught you in.

ANN (*Moving away from him*)   Good afternoon, Mr.
Latham. I was just leaving.

PETER   I'll take you home.

ANN (*Conscious of* MRS. MARGOLIN's *curious gaze*)   No,
thank you, I'm . . . (*To* MRS. MARGOLIN) This is Mr.
Latham. Mr. Latham is . . . is . . .

PETER (*Helps* MRS. MARGOLIN *with her coat*)   Looking for
a studio apartment.

ANN (*Sits at the desk*)   Yes. That's right. I'll take care of it,
Mrs. Margolin. You go along.

MRS. MARGOLIN (*Suspiciously*)   I see. (*Takes her bag, and
goes to the door*) Don't forget you've got an appointment
tonight. With Mr. Edwards.

ANN   I won't forget.

MRS. MARGOLIN   I see.
(*She goes. There is a moment of silence*)

PETER (*Moving toward her*)   Penelope. Penelope Schwartz.
(ANN *smiles, and gives a small shrug*) That's a pretty
strong defense. Give a guy the wrong name and number
so that when he doesn't call, it's because he couldn't, not
because he didn't want to.

ANN (*Smiles*) Did you really try to find Miss Schwartz? It never occurred to me that you would.

PETER Why did you cut out? The next morning you disappeared. You just cut out.

ANN I'm sorry. But now you see why. I mean, among other things, I am the mother of a grown daughter.

PETER Let's have dinner.

ANN Peter, you're very sweet, but I can't have dinner with you. I can't see you again.

PETER Look, there's no button on my lapel: "STANLEY REALTY SLEEPS AROUND."

ANN (*Rises*) Now please listen to me. This entire situation is . . . is just horribly embarrassing.

PETER Let's have dinner.

ANN (*Turns to him*) Peter. I can't be seen running around with a . . . (*Smiles ruefully*) You're just a kid. I could be arrested.

PETER (*Grins*) Risk it.

ANN (*Moving away from him*) You've got to understand my position.

PETER I do. I understand your position.

ANN Then you must realize why I can't see you again. I'm sorry, but that's the way it is.

PETER I see.

ANN I'm really sorry.

PETER I'm sorry, too.

ANN   Thank you, Peter. You're very understanding. (*Holds out her hand*) Goodbye, Peter.
(PETER *takes her hand.* MAUD *enters in a flurry with umbrella and raincoat.* ANN *takes her hand away*)

MAUD   It's a cloudburst! I was on my way from . . . (*Sees* PETER; *lights up*) Why, Peter Latham! How nice to see you.
(*He goes to her; they shake hands*)

PETER   Hello, Mrs. Hayes. That's a very dashing raincoat.

MAUD   I'm *so* glad you like it. It's Trina's . . . What are you doing here?

ANN   Mr. Latham is . . .

PETER   I'm looking for an apartment.

ANN   Yes.

PETER   I thought Mrs. Stanley might be able to help me.

ANN   Unfortunately, I haven't *a thing to offer him.*

MAUD (*Very cordial*)   But how nice of you to come to Ann.

PETER   Natural selection.

MAUD   That's sweet.
(ANN *glowers at* PETER)

MAUD   I've been to the hairdresser. Rain! Wouldn't you know? Naturally, not a taxi in sight. I guess we'll just have to sit it out.
(*She sits in the chair in front of the desk*)

ANN   Mother, I can't wait. I have an appointment and I have to change. So let's make a dash for the subway.

MAUD   The subway!

PETER I have my car here.

MAUD (*Adoringly*) Aren't you marvelous!

ANN (*Goes to the file, and picks up her bag. To* PETER) Absolutely marvelous. But I don't want to take you out of your way . . .

MAUD (*Cutting in firmly*) Now I'm sure Mr. Latham . . .

PETER Peter.

MAUD (*Smiling cozily*) Peter . . . wouldn't mind dropping us off. Especially if we ask him up for tea.

PETER Why, I'd love to.

ANN (*Cutting in sharply*) Mother, I told you I . . .

MAUD (*Airily rises, goes to* PETER, *and takes his right arm*) Oh, yes, you have an appointment. Well, then, Trina and I will have to look after Peter. (*To* PETER) Trina will be delighted to see you.
     (ANN *sits wearily in the chair in front of the desk*)

PETER I'm sure she will. I owe her seventeen dollars. She hustled me in a poolroom. Well . . . my car's parked right outside. (*He takes* MAUD *to the door. She picks up her umbrella*) It's the little red Maserati.

MAUD A Maserati . . . Ah, la dolce vita!
     (*She goes*)

PETER (*Goes to the coatrack, and gets her coat and scarf*) Come on. Let's go.

ANN (*Rises*) Peter, I do not want you to come to my apartment.

PETER I promised your mother.

ANN This is ridiculous, Peter, and I . . .
 (PETER *begins to bundle her into her coat*)

PETER Left. Your *left* arm . . . (ANN *is forced to change her purse from the left hand to the right*) That's a girl . . .

ANN You cannot behave like this!

PETER Do you really have a date tonight?

ANN Yes, I do.
 (*He starts buttoning her up, doing so incorrectly. She pulls away from him, and begins fumbling with the buttons*)

PETER Who have you got a date with?

ANN Please! I can button my own coat!
 (*She goes toward the door.* PETER *follows*)

PETER Who have you got a date with?

ANN (*Stops, and turns to him, very determined, more than a little angry*) Now, Peter. We're going out to the car. And you're going to drive Mother and me home. Then you're going to say you just remembered an appointment you forgot, and you're going to excuse yourself. You will then say goodbye and drive away into the sunset in your little red Maserati. You will definitely not come up. You are not to telephone me, you are not to come to this office again, and (*She goes through the door, but her voice is still heard*) you will never again come to my apartment . . .

PETER (*As he goes*) We'll talk about it up at your place.

 (*There is a blackout. Then rock-'n'-roll music is heard*)

30

The scene is ANN's *apartment, a little later.* PETER *is sitting in the desk chair. He rises, reaches for an ouzo bottle on the bar and looks at it.* TRINA *enters from the hall. He puts down the bottle.*

TRINA   Hi! What brought you?

PETER   I just happened to meet your grandmother and she invited me up.

TRINA   Oh.
(MAUD *enters from the kitchen*)

PETER   Mrs. Hayes, I see you've got some ouzo.

MAUD   Oh, that's a ghastly drink.

TRINA (*To* PETER)   Mummy's been hooked on it ever since she and Granny got back from Greece.

PETER (*Pleased*)   Oh?

MAUD (*Hates the thought of Greece*)   Do you know Greece?

PETER   A little.

TRINA   Granny hated it.

MAUD   I couldn't bear the food. All that oil.

PETER   I know. It can give you a fantastically upset stomach.

MAUD   Exactly! Well, I must make a phone call. (*Sig-*

31

nificantly to TRINA) I'm sure you young people can get along without me for a moment. You two must have a lot to talk about.

    (*She pushes* TRINA *toward* PETER, *and goes*)

TRINA (*After a beat*)   You owe me . . .
    (*She puts out her hand*)

PETER (*Takes the money from his pocket*) Seventeen bucks.
    (*He hands her the money*)

TRINA (*Counts it, and slips it into her boot*) Poor concentration. That's your trouble.
    (*She slouches on the sofa*)

PETER (*Slouches in a chair on the right*) Mmmm. Pretty wet out today.

TRINA   Yeah. All day.

PETER   I don't mind rain.

TRINA   Rain's okay.

PETER   So, what's new since the other night?

TRINA   Nothing much. What's new with you?

PETER   Nothing. (*Rising*) Well, it's nice talking to you.

TRINA   You too.

PETER   Say, where'd you learn to shoot pool like that?

TRINA   My stepfather.

PETER (*A take*)   *Who?*

TRINA   Mummy's second husband.

PETER   Oh.

MAUD (*Entering from the hall*) I just told them they'd have to play without me tonight. I am *not* going out in this weather. (*To* TRINA) Trina, did you know your mother's finding an apartment for Peter?

TRINA   Oh?

MAUD   Well, Peter, will you be living permanently in New York? One always associates your family with Pittsburgh.

TRINA   *Pittsburgh?* Eaacck.

MAUD (*Trying to signal* TRINA)   Trina, dear, you've absolutely no experience with the rich cultural life of regional America. People live very pleasantly indeed outside of New York.

TRINA   In *Pittsburgh?* You couldn't pay me.

MAUD (*Longing to put a hand over* TRINA's *mouth*)   Pittsburgh's *lovely!* (*To* PETER) If I'm not mistaken, your grandparents had that extraordinary house just outside of Pittsburgh . . . What was it called?

PETER   "Belwood."

MAUD   "Belwood!"

PETER   My parents live there now. The Hohenhauser Astrodome.

TRINA (*Not much interested*)   Yeah? If you're so rich, you ought to make Mummy get you one of those sexy apartments at River House.

MAUD   Trina, I'm sure Peter has told your mother exactly what he wants.

PETER   Exactly. (*Looks at his watch*) I wanted to talk it over with her. How long do you think she'll be?

33

TRINA (*With a shrug*)   She's getting dressed.

MAUD   Trina, do you know who Ann's having dinner with this evening? She's being very mysterious.

TRINA   What's she got to be mysterious about?

MAUD   A beau?

TRINA   Oh, come off it.

PETER   Why do you say that?

TRINA   You don't know my mother. Actually . . . (*Turns her attention directly to* PETER) I mean, you don't have to be diplomatic, but wouldn't you honestly say she was still pretty attractive? I mean for her age?

PETER   Yes, I would.

TRINA   I mean if you were an older man *you'd* find her attractive.

PETER (*Judiciously*)   I believe I would. Yes.

TRINA   Well, she wouldn't find *you* attractive.

MAUD   Trina! How can you be so rude!

TRINA   Oh, Granny Maud, I'm just trying to say that Mummy doesn't find *anybody* attractive. She *refuses* to find anybody attractive. Two divorces and she's out of business.

MAUD   Trina, I don't think Peter is interested in . . .

PETER (*He is very interested*)   Go on.

TRINA   So she just *doesn't*. If you know what I mean.

MAUD (*Laughs as though it were a joke*)   Trina! (ANN *enters from the bedroom, wearing a short dinner dress.*

She looks very glamorous. Both TRINA *and* MAUD *are impressed and somewhat mystified.* ANN *crosses to the coffee table, and picks up a cigarette)* That's *new.*

TRINA   Not bad.

ANN (*Quite pleased with herself*)   Do you like it?

MAUD   It's lovely!

TRINA   Yeah, it's really okay. Peter, tell her it's okay.

PETER   It's okay!

MAUD   Isn't it a little too short?
(ANN *is instantly filled with doubt about the dress*)

PETER (*Passionately*)   No! (*All three women turn to stare at him. He reddens*) I mean . . . it looks perfect. To *me.* It really does. *Perfect.*
(*He moves toward* ANN *a bit too quickly, thrusting the flame of his cigarette lighter at her. She allows him to light her cigarette, then turns away*)

MAUD   My goodness, who's all this for?

TRINA   Who rates the parade?

ANN (*Unnerved by all this scrutiny*)   Well, really! Must you two act as if I spend all my evenings schlumping around in snowshoes!

MAUD   You're obviously out to overwhelm somebody! Who?

ANN   I have a *business* date with a Mr. Edwards. (*Nervously stubs out her cigarette in an ashtray by the sofa.* PETER *starts to cross the room toward her. She avoids him*) What time is it?

PETER   Six forty-five.

MAUD   Don't be nervous.

ANN   I am not at all nervous!
(*She takes another cigarette*)

MAUD   You know how traffic is.
(*Again* PETER *moves swiftly in to light it. He startles her. She yelps*)

ANN   Stop creeping up on me!
(*The doorbell rings*)

TRINA (*Starts for the door*)   Shall I go?

ANN   I'll go. (TRINA *stops, rather startled at* ANN's *vehemence.* ANN *starts toward the door.* MAUD, TRINA *and* PETER *stare in fascination.* ANN, *at the door, turns and sees them*) What is the *matter* with you? Will you please relax? (MAUD *and* TRINA *sit on the left of the sofa,* PETER *follows, sits on the right of the sofa. Each tries to think of something to say*) Talk among yourselves!
(ANN *opens the door.* EDDY EDWARDS *appears*)

MAUD   I had the craziest poker game Thursday night. There was Mrs. Peterson, Mrs. Tillit and Mrs. Bayard . . . *Cynthia* Bayard . . .

ANN (*To* EDDY)   Hello.

EDDY (*Taking in* ANN's *appearance*)   Wow! (*The three people stop speaking when they hear* EDDY, *and turn in unison to regard him*) When you pull yourself together, baby, you really get everything in the right place!
(*He looks at the three on the sofa*)

ANN (*A small nervous laugh*)   Come in . . . come in . . .
(*She closes the door*)

EDDY (*Looking around the apartment*)   Very nice. You

really do have the touch. (*Looks at the trio on the sofa*) Oh, say, I . . .

ANN   I'm afraid we're . . . (*As one,* PETER, TRINA *and* MAUD *rise*) . . . it's a bit of a family evening, Mr. Edwards . . .

EDDY (*Delighted*)   I like that!

ANN   Mother, may I present Mr. Edwards . . . My mother, Mrs. Hayes.

MAUD   My daughter has talked so much about you, Mr. Edwards.

EDDY (*Pleased*)   Is that a fact?

ANN   And this is my daughter, Trina . . .

TRINA   How do you do, Mr. Edwards.

EDDY   Hello, young lady . . . Looks seem to run in the family . . . (*Turns to* PETER) And this is your son.
        (ANN *blinks, utterly taken aback*)

EDDY   Hi there, fella!

PETER   I'm Peter Latham.

MAUD   Peter is a friend of my granddaughter's, Mr. Edwards.

EDDY   Natural mistake. (*To* ANN) He's handsome enough to be yours.

ANN (*Drily*)   Thank you. Something to drink, Eddy?

EDDY (*Sits in a chair*)   Bourbon . . . rocks . . . no water . . . (ANN *furiously motions for the three to sit, then starts mixing the drink at the bar*) It's great to be around a family together like this . . . my wife died a year ago.

ANN   I'm so sorry. I didn't know.

MAUD   My daughter tells me you've just acquired a marvelous new apartment.

TRINA   And very expensive. I hear Mummy clipped you.
(ANN *goes to* EDDY, *and gives him the drink*)

EDDY (*Laughs good-naturedly*)   That's right, kid. And I loved it. A dinky little apartment and this pretty little lady looks you straight in the eye and says two hundred, and you know she means big ones.

ANN   That's high-class clipping.

EDDY   You're going to have to throw in some free advice. Give me a couple of hints about drapes and chintz and all that shit . . .
(*He realizes what he has said, and blushes furiously*)

ANN (*Consolingly to* EDDY)   I have never heard the decorating business more accurately described.
(*She goes into the bedroom.* EDDY *gulps down his drink*)

MAUD (*Social manner*)   Has the rain let up, Mr. Edwards?

EDDY (*Gratefully*)   A bit.

MAUD   You stay, Peter. You can join us for a *petit diner*.
(PETER *smiles; looks at Trina; hesitates*)

PETER   Well . . .

TRINA   It's okay, Pete. You can stay if you want.
(*She puts her feet up on the coffee table, gets a furious look from* MAUD, *which she ignores*)

PETER   Thanks, I'd like to.

TRINA   And later we can shoot some pool at McGirr's.

EDDY (*With interest*)   A little girl like you shooting pool?

PETER (*To* EDDY)   She just *looks* like a girl. She's really Paul Newman.
(ANN *returns carrying a purse and gloves*)

ANN   I'm ready.

EDDY (*On his feet*)   Then I guess we're off. But I sure hate to leave all these nice people . . .

ANN (*A hard look at the trio*)   Well, *I* don't. (*Goes to the sofa*) Good night, Mother . . . Trina. *Goodbye,* Peter.

PETER (*Cheerfully*)   Oh, I'll probably be here when you get back.
(*He puts his legs up on the coffee table*)

MAUD   Trina, take your feet off the table.

ANN (*To* PETER)   You, too.
(*They comply.* ANN *goes toward the door*)

EDDY   Mrs. Hayes, it's been good talking to you. Good night, young lady. So long, son.
(*He points his index finger at* PETER, *very buddy-buddy.* PETER *imitates*)

PETER   Sir.
(ANN *opens the door, disclosing* BILLY *on the threshold, a bag of Chinese food in cartons in his arms*)

BILLY   I was just about to ring. I'm not too late?

ANN   About eight years.

BILLY   You invited me to dinner.

ANN   I said call me Wednesday, and if it's convenient we can have dinner together.

BILLY   This is outrageous! I brought Moo Goo Gai Pan. You *love* Moo Goo Gai Pan.
   (*He shoves the bag into her hand*)

EDDY   Uh . . . Mrs. Stanley . . . if you really had a date with your beau . . .

ANN   He's not my beau, and I did *not* have a date with him. He's just a . . . part-time ex-husband.

EDDY (*Puzzled*)   Oh.

BILLY (*Goes to* EDDY, *near the bar, his hand outstretched genially*)   Billy Boylan.

EDDY   Eddy Edwards. (*Instantly recognizing the name, then the face, he begins to beam. He takes the proffered hand, and shakes it enthusiastically*) Billy Boylan. I've seen you! On *Peyton Place*! (*To* ANN) Billy Boylan!

ANN (*Wearily*)   Billy Boylan. (*To* EDDY) Eddy, let's go.

BILLY (*To* ANN)   You're seriously going to dump me to-night?

MAUD (*Gets up, and takes the bag from* ANN)   If you're feeling abandoned, Billy, you can stay with us. *We'll* eat your Moo Goo Gai Pan.
   (*She starts for the kitchen*)

EDDY   Listen . . . you know it just seems like a shame to go off and leave a party.
   (*When she hears the word "party,"* MAUD *stops*)

ANN (*Protesting sincerely*)   Oh, please!

EDDY (*Goes to* ANN *at the door*)   I've got an idea . . . I'll get the driver to hurry over to the Caviarteria . . . caviar . . . smoked turkey . . . salmon . . .

MAUD   Be sure it's fresh caviar.

EDDY   Sure!

BILLY   Wine! We'll need wine.

EDDY   Right! We'll have a real party. Right *here!* Okay?
Okay?

BILLY   Marvy!

MAUD   Lovely!
        (ANN *stands frustrated, furious*)

ANN   Swell!

EDDY   I'll be right back! (*He stops, and turns with a broad,
    happy smile*) Billy Boylan!
        (*He goes*)

BILLY (*To* MAUD)   What a darling guy.

TRINA   He's nice.

MAUD   And very *generous.*

ANN (*To* PETER, *glowering at him*)   I do hope *you* like him.
        (*She goes into the bedroom to put away her purse
        and gloves*)

BILLY   Hey there, Granny Maud, we'll do the table.

MAUD (*As she goes for the kitchen*)   Salmon and caviar.
    I'll get the pink plates.
        (*She goes*)

TRINA (*Heading for her room*)   I'm going to change.
        (*She goes*)

BILLY (*Who has started for the kitchen, now notices* PETER,
    turns back)   You're . . .

PETER   Peter Latham.

ANN *(Entering from the bedroom)*   *Trina's* friend.

BILLY   Hello, Peter. Billy Boylan.
(They shake hands)

PETER   Billy Boylan.

BILLY *(Going toward the kitchen)*   Well, let's get this show on the road. *(Turns back)* Glad to have you aboard, Pete.

PETER   Thanks. (BILLY *exits, leaving* ANN *and* PETER *alone for a moment. She starts toward the kitchen)* How about you, Ann?

ANN   What about me?

PETER *(Goes to her)*   Are *you* glad to have me aboard?

ANN *(Stops)*   What?

PETER   Are *you* glad to have me aboard? *(He kisses her. She starts to respond, then suddenly pushes him away, and looks at him thoughtfully)* Answer me!

ANN *(Weakly)*   What was the question?

(There is a blackout. Then fast gypsy music is heard)

SCENE SIX

The scene is ANN'*s apartment, the next day, Sunday. It is about five o'clock in the afternoon. A football game is on the television. We hear the sound of a band at half-time.*

BILLY'*s jacket is on a chair. On the sofa in his shirt-sleeves, and wearing an apron lies* BILLY, *sound asleep. The TV set is on his stomach.* TRINA *comes out of her room dressed to go out. She imitates a drum majorette with a baton.*

TRINA   Hey, Billy, tell Mummy I've gone.
> (BILLY *does not waken.* TRINA *shuts off the TV, and puts it on the end table.* BILLY *wakes up, startled*)

BILLY   Don't do that! I'm watching the game.

TRINA   It's half-time. You were sleeping.

BILLY   Resting. That damned party last night.

TRINA   You look very sweet in that apron.

BILLY (*Sits up*)   Pucci. Ann lured me into this by saying, "Come on over and finish up the caviar."

TRINA   I finished it this morning.

BILLY   I noticed. What Ann meant was, "Come on over and finish the dishes."

TRINA   'Bye.
> (ANN *enters from the kitchen, carrying a tray with ice bucket and liquor*)

ANN   The dishes are done. (*To* TRINA) Where are you off to?

TRINA   To the flicks with some kids. 'Bye, Billy. (*Archly*) You were absolutely dazzling last night. The competition from Eddy must have stimulated you.
(*She exits*)

BILLY   Trina's such a little bitch, I can't believe she's not my own daughter.

ANN (*Moving toward the sofa*)   Well, Billy, you *were* pretty dazzling last night. Boy, were you dazzling. Hup!
(*She snaps her fingers. He raises his legs as she slides under them. Comfortably ensconced, she then places her own legs across his. This is obviously an old routine with them. They are very cozy*)

BILLY   My God, what a scene! (*Sighs*) Dancing the night away. *Me* with Granny Maud.

ANN (*Starts to eat an apple*)   Nobody forced you.

BILLY   *Eddy* forced me. I didn't want to go on the town. Eddy *forced* me. He insisted. He *wanted* me. (*Imitating* EDDY) Billy boy, Mrs. Hayes, little lady, sonny . . . We're going on the town. The party's on Big Ed. (*Back to normal*) He wanted me.

ANN   He *wanted* to be polite. He *wanted* to make a good impression on *me*. That's what he wanted. But you and Mother . . .

BILLY   Why pick on Maud and me? Trina and young Peter certainly stayed the course. (*Pause*) He's quite an attractive boy, isn't he?

ANN (*Starts to take a bite of apple, then stops*)   No.

BILLY   No? I thought he was quite attractive. Very poised.

ANN   He's not attractive to *me*.

BILLY   I thought he was very attractive. Very poised.

ANN   He's too poised.

BILLY   Is he Trina's new thing?

ANN   What else?

BILLY   Oh, I don't know. (*Joking*) Maybe as Mama gets older, she fancies 'em younger.

ANN (*Furious*)   What a filthy little showbiz mind . . .
         (*She takes one of his moccasins off and starts to go for him with it*)

BILLY   Hey. Hey. (*He takes the shoe from her gently but firmly, puts it on her foot*) Wait a minute! I'm *sorry*.

ANN   You can be the most tasteless . . .

BILLY   Sorry . . .

ANN   There's nothing in the world more revolting than a creaky old lady running after a boy.

BILLY (*Kindly*)   Come on. You're only thirty-eight.

ANN (*Mumbles into the apple*)   Forty.

BILLY   What?

ANN (*Speaks right out this time*)   Forty.

BILLY (*Starts to rise with interest*)   Forty! You mean you're older than *me*?

ANN   You're forty-*one*.

BILLY   *Thirty-eight!* It's in Celebrity Register. Thirty-eight. (*Traces numbers in the air with his finger*) Three-eight. (*She stares fixedly, accusingly at him. He sighs, shrugs*) Forty-two.

ANN   Forty-*two?*

BILLY   Forget it! (ANN *leans back, delighted*) Anyway, I like that Eddy. He suits me fine. I like him.

ANN   I'm glad. If I ever run into him again I'll tell him.

BILLY   (*Rises to a sitting position, and puts on his shoe.* ANN *sits up*) Don't kid a kidder, baby. You're seeing him tonight. I *heard.*

ANN   (*Laughs*)   What's it to you?

BILLY   It's time you found somebody to take care of you. Somebody substantial, like Eddy. I wouldn't want you screwing around with some little penny-ante adventurer.

ANN   (*Sincerely*)   Billy, I want you to know how much I truly appreciate your not minding your own business.

BILLY   Stick with me, kid. *And* if the chance presents itself, you might slip in a kind word for little Billy.
(*He rises, takes off the apron, and puts it on the coffee table*)

ANN   (*Still kidding*)   I'll try to find one.

BILLY   (*Suddenly serious*)   I'm not kidding. I need it.

ANN   (*Astonished*)   You're not having trouble getting work, are you?

BILLY   (*Starts to put on his jacket*)   Not at all, I'm not pushing Richard Burton off the screen, but I think I'll probably survive him.

ANN   Then *what?*

BILLY   Annie, the most extraordinary, the most unaccountable . . . *sensations* have been zapping me for the last year . . .

46

ANN (*Deeply concerned*)   What *is* it?

BILLY   It comes over me at the damnedest times . . . on the set, the cameras grinding away, my nose down some stupid bird's bozoom . . . Suddenly I hear this voice: "Is this any way for a grown man to make a living?" Or I'm horsing around with the gang in Vegas. Everybody's having a million laughs. And suddenly I find myself wondering if I wouldn't rather be home with a book . . . I mean a home with an upstairs and a wife and a kid with remedial reading. I tell you, at first I thought I was losing my effing mind! Annie, I've been putting on make-up and wearing elevator shoes for over twenty years. Now, suddenly, for *no reason,* it embarrasses me. I want to give up acting and go straight.

ANN   *You?* Give up acting? You're too good!

BILLY (*Thoughtfully pauses, then admits*)   True. But . . .

ANN (*Bewildered*)   What on earth could you *do?*

BILLY (*Goes to* ANN)   Well, I thought maybe Eddy . . . Annie, I want to try to get a job. I mean a real job.

ANN   Like what?

BILLY   Public relations?

ANN (*Dubiously*)   Public relations? Is that real?

BILLY (*Crossly*)   I've got to start somewhere. What do you want me to do, go cold turkey? (*Starts for the bar*) I think I'll have a drink.

ANN (*Shakes her head*)   No. You're going home.

BILLY (*Stops*)   Why?

ANN (*Rises, and starts for the bedroom*)   Because I'm

tireder than I thought. I want a little rest before Eddy gets here.

BILLY   Ah. I accept that. Make yourself gorgeous. You know, that couple of pounds you put on during your vacation are very nicely distributed. Eddy looks like a guy who would go for the curves.

ANN   Billy, a forty-year-old woman doesn't need a stage mother.

BILLY   Forty years old! Don't think like that—think like a diamond.

ANN   Huh?

BILLY   Not years—carats. You are a multi-carated, blue-white . . .
   (*The phone rings*)

ANN   Ah! ! That must be Harry Winston now! (*The phone rings again. She answers it. Into the phone*) Hello? . . . Oh, *Eddy!* (BILLY *sits at the desk chair. She immediately takes his arm, and pushes him to the sofa. He sits on the right arm of the sofa*) . . . Oh, I did too. The party was just marvelous. And wildly extravagant. What time tonight? (*Listens for a moment, her face falling*) Oh, I see. Well, if you can't make it, you can't.

BILLY   (*Rises, goes to her, speaks sotto voce*)   What's he trying to pull?

ANN   (*Covers the mouthpiece*)   Don't be such a pimp! (*Into the phone*) What about tomorrow? . . . Oh, for the whole week? (BILLY *sits again*) Well, have a good trip . . . Please don't apologize! I'll talk to you when you get back . . . Goodbye.
   (*She hangs up*)

BILLY   The balloon go up?

ANN   He's been called to the Coast on business. You surely
don't want him to neglect *your future!* (*Shrugs*) I'll fix
you something to eat.

BILLY (*Looks at his watch*)   Well, actually, Ann . . .

ANN   Are *you* going to walk out on me too?

BILLY (*Sincerely*)   I've got a goddamn date.
(*He rises*)

ANN   I should know better than to count on you for anything.

BILLY   Honey, I've had this date all week!

ANN   So who's the lucky girl?

BILLY   Elke.

ANN   Elke . . .

BILLY   You remember Elke.

ANN   Elke? Who works upstairs? That big blond knockwurst?

BILLY   That *gorgeous* big blond knockwurst.

ANN   Billy, it's very disrespectful for you to sleep with the
help in *my building.* This is a *co-op* (*Sits down*) And
since you're now so adult, you really ought to give up
mother's helpers. I see her in the elevator all the time.
She lets the kid's nose run! She looks feeble-minded.
She's a minor. How old is she, anyway?

BILLY   Almost nineteen.

ANN   That's rotten!

49

BILLY What is?

ANN You are seducing an underaged, feeble-minded, Kindersitter! *Why?*

BILLY (*Thoughtfully*) She don't fight back.

ANN (*Laughs*) You old goat.
(*She throws a pillow at him*)

BILLY (*Tosses the pillow on the sofa*) Part of the growing-up process I was describing to you is this marvelous goatish thing for helpless young girls. This must be maturity.
(*He crosses to the door*)

ANN (*Grins*) Oh, Billy, beat it. Everything's so utterly ridiculous.

BILLY (*He opens the door, starts to go, then pokes his head back in*) I really am sorry about tonight.
(*He goes*)

ANN Okay. Okay. Okay. (*She rises*) Okay . . .
(*She replaces the pillow on the chair, goes to the bar, picks up the bottle of ouzo, puts it back, starts to hum the Greek theme melody, does a wistful little dance step toward the sofa, picks up an apple, eats it to console herself as she lies down, turns on the television set listlessly, reaches over, turns on a lamp. We hear less than half a minute of the Pan-Am jingle: "Pan-Am makes the going great," etc., then the* ANNOUNCER'S VOICE *is heard*)

ANNOUNCER'S VOICE Yes, Pan-Am makes the going great. Go with Pan-Am and you'll go where the action is. This is the blue Aegean with its lovely, romantic islands. Let a

Pan-Am ticket take you there. Go where the action is. Go where it's happening. Go! Go! Go!

ANN (*Snapping off the set*) I went! (*She sighs. The door-bell rings. She goes to the door, and opens it. It is* PETER. ANN *starts to shut the door. He pushes back*) You can't force your way in here . . .

PETER For Chrissake, Ann, this is so bloody *undignified* . . .

ANN Please. I'm not alone. (*She turns, backs up against the door, and hisses at him*) Mother's in her room.

PETER No she's not. (*Pushes his way in*) I saw her go out just past noon. *And* Trina. I've been waiting hours for that bastard Boylan to leave. Where did he go?

ANN He's got a girl friend in the building.

PETER (*Looks at her questioningly*) Do you care?

ANN I just didn't expect to have to spend the evening alone.

PETER Well, now you don't.
(ANN *looks at him thoughtfully; closes the door; makes up her mind to attempt reason*)

ANN Peter . . . sit down, Peter. I want to talk to you.

PETER Okay. I want to talk to you, too.
(*He sits on the right end of the sofa*)

ANN Now, Peter. This has got to stop. You know that. You are a very intelligent boy. You're even a rather sensitive boy. You have a way of . . . a kind of natural authority that is . . .
(*She is reaching for a word*)

PETER (*Helping*) Very unusual.

ANN   Very unusual in a . . .

PETER (*Continuing to feed her*)   In a lad of my years.

ANN (*Picking it up*)   . . . in a lad of your . . . *Don't mock me.* (*He puts his left leg comfortably up on the sofa*) Now, Peter. Since you are intelligent *and* sensitive . . . you must have some *small* . . . some small . . .
         (*Again, she is reaching for a word*)

PETER and ANN (*Together*)   Insight.

ANN   Yes. Some small insight into my position . . . (*She sits on the left end of the sofa, and starts to put her legs over his, as she had done previously with* BILLY. *She is horrified as she realizes her error, and immediately puts her feet back on the floor and sits up very straight*) my feelings. It must be obvious . . . at least I *hope* it is . . . that I am a respectable woman . . . (PETER *reaches for her hand. She moves away on the sofa. He follows*) I mean I know what happened . . . what happened in Greece . . . *Nevertheless* . . .
         (PETER *leans over and kisses her, firmly but gently, to stem the flow of words. When he moves back, she just sits quietly*)

PETER   May I speak now? Ann . . . (*He rises, moves away, then turns back*) by the time I was ten I'd had four passports. My mother buzzed around a lot and I'll say this for her, she was always ready to yank me along with her. I wasn't left to the servants. My old man's kind of a standard son-of-a-bitch and my mother . . .

ANN   Oh, Peter. I'm sure I remind you of your mother. You may not have been conscious of it, but . . .

PETER   I've never known a woman who reminded me less of my mother. You know who reminds me of my mother? *Trina* reminds me of my mother.

ANN (*Laughs, then turns serious*) Oh, God.

PETER All I'm trying to say is that I'm only twenty-two—

ANN (*Softly*) I know.

PETER —but I've been around. I've had my quota of girls . . . and their mothers . . .

ANN Do you spare the grannies?

PETER You're an astonishingly unsophisticated woman, you know. (*Grins*) Very middle-class . . .

ANN (*A small smile*) You are ridiculous.

PETER You're smiling. That's the first time you've really smiled at me. Do you like for me to be ridiculous? It's easy.

ANN Peter . . . I don't know what to say. I'm very touched and absolutely *horrified*.

PETER Why?

ANN Because I had no idea. Peter, I *cannot* let you come here again.

PETER I think you're right about that. We'll take an apartment . . .
       (*She rises;* PETER *follows*)

ANN Peter . . . I want you to go now.

PETER No, that's not what you want.

ANN I mean it!

PETER (*Casually*) In all the hoo-ha around here, I think I forgot to tell you that I am in love with you.

ANN (*Speechless for a moment*) I'm very honored. And

53

terribly flattered. (*He tries to take her hands. She evades him, moving away. He follows her slowly*) But Peter, for you to be in love with me, it just isn't . . . *convenient.* You can't just . . . *fling* yourself into my life like some crazy . . . sit-in! Every time I move I have to step over you. You're upsetting things. (*Desperately*) My life has a certain . . . a certain balance . . . and harmony—

PETER   You'd be better off with a little chaos.

ANN   Well, you certainly provide that!

PETER   It's the youth bit. (*Smiles engagingly, and goes to her*) Spontaneity. Say what you mean. Mean what you feel. Pow! Action Now. You'll learn to love it.

ANN   No. No, I won't. Don't you understand I've *had* all that . . . that "Pow! Action Now" business. What I want is (*Softly*) "Pow!" . . . *Tranquility* Now.
(*She sits wearily on the arm of the chair*)

PETER   How about trying for "dead"?

ANN   I *mean* it.

PETER   I don't believe you.

ANN   Then believe *this.* I am not attracted to young boys. Not you, not *any.*

PETER   Lady, that is a lie. I don't know about anybody else, but you are certainly attracted to *me.* Why can't you be honest? What are you so frightened of?

ANN   It's horrible!

PETER   What is?

ANN (*Rises, turns away*)   Falling all over a young man . . .

PETER But you're not falling all over me.

ANN (*Turns to him*) Not yet!
  (*Realizes what she has revealed, and turns away
  again*)

PETER Well, that was honest.

ANN *I am not in love with you.*

PETER You don't know whether you are or not. You
  haven't given yourself a chance. You're so spooked by the
  idea of what People Will Think, you can't think yourself. Listen, Ann . . . Whose opinions count so much to
  you? Your mother's? Your daughter's? Pat Nixon's?
  Your mother's charming, but she wouldn't care if I were
  still in short pants as long as she hooks up with the Hohenhausers . . .

ANN Why, you arrogant . . .

PETER (*Going on*) As for Trina . . .

ANN Please go.

PETER You are a beautiful and desirable woman . . .
  (*Goes to her*) I love you, Ann . . . Let me love you.
  (*He takes her in his arms. They embrace*)

ANN (*Pulling away as she hears a key in the front door*)
  Oh, God! It's my mother!
  (*She yanks away from him just in time.* MAUD *enters,
  wearing a coat and hat*)

MAUD (*As usual, delighted to see* PETER) Why, good evening, Peter dear!

PETER Good evening, Mrs. Hayes. I just dropped in . . .

ANN Unfortunately, Trina isn't in.

MAUD (*To* PETER, *teasingly*) But you'll wait for her, won't you?

ANN You mustn't try to keep him, Mother. He's already said he had to leave . . .

MAUD Oh, what a pity. Trina will be utterly shattered at having missed you!

ANN Yes.

PETER (*Shakes her hand*) Good night, Mrs. Hayes. I'm glad I at least got a glimpse of *you* . . . (*To* ANN) Good night.
 (*He goes to the door*)

ANN (*Follows him*) Good night, Peter.

MAUD (*Sits on the sofa, and starts to take off her hat and gloves; unbuttons her coat*) Come back soon. You're part of the family now. We've adopted you!

ANN (*Opening the door*) Good night.
 (PETER *kisses her hand.* MAUD *is not watching; she's busy with her gloves and hat.* PETER *keeps kissing both of* ANN's *hands. She tries to push him out the door, but he playfully keeps kissing her hands. She finally gets him out the door. His hands still show and she's trying to avoid closing the door on them. She keeps pushing his hands the way one does with a cat's paws when trying to put the cat in a traveling box. She finally succeeds in getting his hands outside, and closes the door. She stands facing the door for a moment. She is exhausted*)

MAUD Has he been here long?

ANN What?

56

MAUD   Has he been here long?

ANN   Who?

MAUD   *Peter.*

ANN (*Walking across the room*)   A few minutes.

MAUD   Of course he's courting you like mad!

ANN (*Stops, and looks at her mother*)   Why would he be courting me?

MAUD   Because he's after Trina.

ANN   Oh.

MAUD   I think he's quite smitten with her.

ANN   You do?

MAUD   Why can't that silly Trina stay home occasionally? (*Rises*) Oh, I'm so glad I'm not that age, anymore. Aren't you?
    (*She goes*)

ANN (*Looks in a mirror, sits on the sofa, picks up the apple from the coffee table. Then in a small, childlike voice, sings the "Mouseketeers" song softly to herself, as if unconscious of what she is singing*) "M-I-C, K-E-Y, M-O-U, S-E."
    (*There is a five-count light fade on "mouse," then rock-'n'-roll music is heard*)

The scene is ANN's *apartment, a month later, in the evening.* TRINA *is on the sofa, doing her homework. She is wearing large sunglasses. The radio is playing rock-'n'-roll music very loud.* MAUD *enters from the hall carrying a large basket of flowers. She turns off the radio.*

TRINA   Please don't turn that off. I'm studying.

MAUD   (*Puts the flowers on a small table*)   Trina, I want to talk to you about Peter.

TRINA   Again?

MAUD   (*Sits on the sofa*)   I want to know if you think he's in love with you.

TRINA   (*Shrugs*)   How should I know?

MAUD   If you don't, I can't think who does! Don't you at least have an opinion?

TRINA   In my opinion, Peter is not in love with me.

MAUD   How does he behave when you're alone.

TRINA   We're never alone . . . if you're not here, Mummy is . . . or if we go out, which isn't very often, it's always with Arthur or some other kids.

MAUD   You went dancing night before last . . . at least you dance alone . . . You know, cheek-to-cheek.

TRINA   (*Sincerely curious about the phrase*)   What-to-what?

MAUD   Don't be coarse! Well, at least you talk to each other. What does he talk about?

TRINA (*As if to a child*)   The whole point of the Electric Circus is you don't have to talk. You can't. It's bombs bursting in air!

MAUD (*A grimace*)   Charming.

TRINA   It's super.

MAUD (*A pause; then she sighs, and tries again*)   He brings you home. What happens when he brings you home?

TRINA   Nothing.

MAUD   He doesn't kiss you?

TRINA (*Laughs*)   No.

MAUD   I don't believe it! My word! You don't suppose he's . . . "you-know"?

TRINA (*Casually*)   No, he's not.

MAUD   How can you tell?

TRINA   I asked him.

MAUD (*Horrified*)   You asked him! Why, you little idiot!

TRINA (*Gathers her books from the floor, and rises*)   Granny Maud, I think you ought to just settle down and accept the fact that Peter is not in love with me. You're never going to be related to the Hohenhausers. He doesn't dig me . . . I don't appeal to him.

MAUD   But you're the living image of me!

TRINA   Then *you* don't appeal to him.

MAUD   Nonsense. He adores me. He's just shy. Needs encouragement.

59

TRINA (*Goes to* MAUD; *comforts her*)   Granny, I'm only seventeen. The world is full of attractive and eligible men. I'm not going to push the panic button because one of them doesn't drop dead at my feet.

MAUD   Peter Latham can provide you with every luxury you can think of, and a great many you've never heard of.
(*The doorbell rings*)

TRINA   Saved by the bell!

MAUD (*Rising authoritatively*)   Trina, please go to your room.

TRINA   Why?

MAUD (*Goes to the door*)   That's Peter. And I want to talk to him. If you won't give the poor boy a little help, *I* will.

TRINA (*Shrugs, and starts for her room*)   If I were you, I wouldn't get mixed up in this.
(*She goes.* MAUD *opens the door and* PETER *enters. He hands* MAUD *a pretty box*)

MAUD   Ah . . .

PETER   Hello, Mrs. Hayes. I brought you some marrons glacés.

MAUD (*Fondly*)   You really do spoil us, Peter. Trina's mother adores marrons glacés.

PETER   Oh, does she? I just took a chance that somebody would. (*Moving toward the small table*) She . . . uh . . . hasn't come home yet?

MAUD   No. I'm alone. We can play without a soul to bother us.
(*She moves the flowers to the coffee table*)

PETER   Great. (PETER *indicates the basket of flowers*) Somebody's birthday?

MAUD (*Sits on the right of the small table*)   No, no. That darling Eddy Edwards sent them.

PETER (*Sits across from* MAUD)   Is *he* back again?

MAUD   Just this morning. (*Deals the cards; looks approvingly at* PETER *as she does so*) My, what a good-looking suit. Aren't you grand!

PETER   The old man was in town today. We had lunch.

MAUD   He must be very proud of you. You take your position in the company very seriously. (*Finishes dealing*) Basically, I feel you are a very serious person. (*They begin to play gin rummy*) Wouldn't you say you are?

PETER   About average, I guess.

MAUD   No, much more than average. I'm a very keen judge of character, Peter. Your emotions run *very* deep. (*Looks at him with big knowing eyes*) Poor Peter . . . (*Surprised, He looks up from the cards, and meets her gaze*) I'm not a complete idiot, you know. I've seen through you for quite a while now. (*It's* PETER'S *turn to draw a card, but he is stunned by what* MAUD *has just said. He draws a card from the deck automatically, and keeps drawing cards, which he puts in his hand without looking and without discarding others.* MAUD *doesn't see any of this, and continues speaking*) I know what's going on, Peter . . . why you come here so often. And I know it isn't to play gin rummy with an old lady. (*She smiles knowingly.* PETER *keeps drawing. He now has drawn six or seven cards*) Do you think I'm so old I no longer recognize love when it's right under my nose?
    (*She now looks at* PETER. *He stops drawing*)

61

PETER (*Cautiously*)   What are you getting at, Mrs. Hayes?

MAUD   Just that I know you're in love and that I'm on your side.

PETER (*Quite taken aback*)   You are?

MAUD   And I'll do anything I can to help you. You have my promise.

PETER   Mrs. Hayes! I never dreamed you'd see it like that!

MAUD   Of course Trina is terribly young . . .

PETER   Who?

MAUD   Trina. She's terribly young.

PETER   Ah.

MAUD   I know, I know. She doesn't seem young. It's a very sophisticated generation. Not like when I was that age . . . or even Ann. Ann was . . . I can see your cards . . . Ann was awesomely innocent. Sometimes I think she still is.

PETER   Yes.

MAUD   Ann doesn't see things head-on. What will be hard for her to grasp is that age is not the question here. The question is simply what is best for the two individuals involved. You will have to convince her that marriage is possible. Possible and desirable. (PETER *raps the table with his fingers.* MAUD *jumps*) You're knocking?

PETER   No. No, you were talking about marriage.

MAUD   Of course. If you really love her.

PETER   Oh, I do love her, Mrs. Hayes. But, marriage! . . . It simply never occurred to me.

MAUD   Peter, I'm shocked!

PETER   Well, there are—uh—obstacles—you know.

MAUD   You're worried about your parents. That they'll think you're too young.

PETER (*Slight grimace*)   Well . . .

MAUD (*Leans toward* PETER)   Can't you bring them around?

PETER (*Leans toward* MAUD, *and grins*)   It would be interesting to try. But I'm not dependent on my parents.

MAUD   However, it would be so much nicer if they did approve.

PETER   So much nicer.

MAUD   Still, every couple must eventually live for themselves. Take a card.

PETER   You believe that?

MAUD   Yes. And you must be very firm with *Ann!* She may fight you.

PETER   I'll handle Ann.

MAUD   And, Peter dear, let me give you just one more bit of advice . . .
   (ANN *enters*)

ANN   I'm home.

MAUD   Gin! (*Slaps her cards face down.* PETER *stares at* MAUD's *cards on the table, and starts to say something.* MAUD *cuts him off. She rises, and messes up all the cards on the table*) It's gin. In spades, and that counts double. If you'll excuse me, I have to go and make up the menus.

We can settle up later, Peter. I know I can trust you. (*As if just now noticing* ANN) Why hello, Ann.
  (*She exits into the hallway*)

ANN   What's she up to? (PETER *is staring at the cards in his hand*) That's a very funny look. What's it supposed to mean?

PETER (*Looking at the cards strangely*)   I've got seventeen cards!
  (*He puts them down*)

ANN (*Goes to the coffee table, picks up the flowers, and puts them back on the card table*)   La! What a splendid suit! (*Teasing*) Playing grown-up?

PETER (*Unflappable*)   About the same as everybody else. When did the Big Wind from the West blow back in?

ANN   Ah! That's what's eating you.

PETER   I just asked if you'd seen the Big Wind.
  (ANN *picks up the box of marrons glacés, turns to him, and smiles. He smiles back. She puts down the marrons, and sits on the sofa*)

ANN   Would you mind fixing me a drink?

PETER (*Goes to the bar, looks toward the hallway to be sure* MAUD *is out of earshot*)   You're pretty late.

ANN (*Tiredly*)   Oh, there were a million rotten things at the office.

PETER (*At the bar, mixing the drink*)   Why do you do it?

ANN (*Annoyed*)   Why do I . . . I've got bad habits. I like to eat.

PETER (*A beat*)   You could get married.

ANN   I've been married.

PETER (*Casually*)   Not to me.

ANN (*Looks at him briefly, and decides to make a joke of it*)   I can't marry you, Peter. It's against the teachings of my church.

PETER (*Goes to her*)   The teachings of what church?

ANN   The Over-Thirty Orthodox.

PETER (*Hands her the drink*)   I'm not kidding, Ann. I'm asking you. Will you marry me?

ANN   I'm not kidding, Peter. I'm telling you. No.

PETER (*Quietly*)   Why?

ANN   Because I know what would happen.

PETER   What would happen?

ANN   You know how old I am.

PETER (*Turns away impatiently*)   Oh God. Look. Suppose you were thirty-five. Would you marry me if you were thirty-five?
            (*He moves in behind her*)

ANN   No.

PETER   Thirty?

ANN   No.

PETER   Twenty-nine?

ANN (*Starts to say no; stops*)   I don't think so . . . no, of course I wouldn't.

PETER   Twenty-five?

ANN (*Hesitates, then smiles*)   I'd be tempted.

PETER   You know you would.

ANN   I might.

PETER   So let's suppose you're twenty-five and we get married. Then what happens?

ANN (*Sharply*)   How do *I* know?

PETER (*Leans toward her*)   Exactly.

ANN (*Puzzled, then annoyed*)   How does anyone know what will happen in a marriage . . . or in life?

PETER   Exactly. (ANN *slowly begins to understand what he's trying to say*) All anybody ever really has is *now*.
(*There is a moment of silence, then* ANN *takes a deep breath*)

ANN (*Starts for the bedroom; turns, and heads for the kitchen*)   Peter, please go. This is my night to . . . (*Reaching*) I've really got to polish the silver.

PETER (*Follows her; takes her shoulders, and gently turns her around to face him*)   All right. But while you're polishing the silver, will you think about it? And try to think about yourself. Nobody else.

ANN (*Still bewildered*)   I'll try.
(*He kisses her, goes up to the door, and turns back*)

PETER   Okay, go on. Polish the silver.
(*He goes.* ANN *stands there lost in thought for a moment.* MAUD, *followed by* TRINA, *enters from the hallway*)

MAUD   Did I hear Peter leave? What did he say?

TRINA What did Peter say to you?

ANN (*Puzzled*) About what?

TRINA I guess you know that Granny practically put a shotgun in his back!

ANN (*Stares at* MAUD) Mother! What on earth did you say to him?

MAUD (*Very pleased with herself*) I simply brought it to his attention that his feelings were perfectly obvious to me and that I thoroughly approved. And I said I wanted to know his intentions.

ANN Oh, you did.

MAUD He was surprised.

ANN He was surprised.

MAUD But when I said I thought he should speak to you, he very quickly agreed. (*Silence*) Well? What happened? Did he declare himself?

ANN He *certainly did*.

TRINA Look, Mummy . . .

MAUD (*Stopping her, impatiently*) Please be quiet, Trina. I'm trying to talk to your mother about Peter.

TRINA It's not *you* he wants to marry, Granny. It's *me*.

ANN (*Gazes from* MAUD *to* TRINA) Actually . . . actually . . . (*Goes to the end of the sofa*) What he's got in mind is something in between—a kind of . . . *compromise*. (*Sits down*) Well, let's put it this way . . .

Fast curtain

Gretchen Corbett as TRINA STANLEY, Julie Harris as ANN STANLEY, and Glenda Farrell as MAUD HAYES

ACT TWO

The scene is ANN's *apartment, a few days later. It is eve-ning.* ANN *and* EDDY *are alone.* ANN, *wearing a kaftan-style robe, is demonstrating different colors and swatches of fabric for* EDDY.

ANN (*Dramatically throwing first one, then another large sample of fabric across the back of the sofa*)   Which do you like? The plum? Or the aubergine?

EDDY (*Stares blankly at the samples*)   Uh . . . Which is the plum and which is the aubergine?

ANN   *This* is the aubergine. *I* like the plum.

EDDY (*Sycophantically*)   I like the plum. It's perfect! I don't see how you do it! I can't even pick out the right tie. (ANN *gives a little grin. He looks down at the tie he is now wearing, shakes his head*) Oh, I guess you noticed. I al-ways depended on my wife for things like that . . . (*Sighs*) I'm mighty grateful for your advice, Ann. This apartment's sure gonna have your brand on it.

ANN (*Laughs, and sits down on the sofa*)   Oh, Eddy.

EDDY   You've been so nice about the little apartment . . . I wonder how you'd feel about taking on something a shade bigger . . .

ANN   What did you have in mind, Eddy?

EDDY   Something out in the country. Maybe Connecticut. Something you could . . . kind of . . . *expand* in. (*Shyly*)

Something maybe a woman might like. Something, say, *you'd* like. I mean to your *taste.*

(*He turns to her.* ANN *is suddenly extremely uncomfortable*)

ANN   I've changed my mind about the plum.

EDDY   I sure wish you'd hear me out, Ann.

ANN   Although the aubergine . . .

EDDY   I was pretty lost after my wife died.

ANN   Yes, yes, I'm sure you were. But Eddy . . .

EDDY   I don't want you to misunderstand me. I'm not trying to pass myself off as something special . . . Matter of fact, I guess if my wife hadn't been sick . . . all those years . . . I would have cut out.

ANN   It must have been very hard on you.

EDDY (*Sits next to her on the sofa, and shrugs*)   Oh, well. You just do what you have to. But, that's all finished and done. Ann . . .

(*He takes her hand. The kitchen door opens and* MAUD *appears*)

MAUD   Ann, do we want that casserole . . (*Sees* ANN *and* EDDY) Oh, Eddy, I didn't know you were still here . . . (*Goes toward the hallway, obviously eager to leave* ANN *and* EDDY *alone*) Oh, please, don't let me disturb you. Continue! Continue!

(EDDY *rises politely.* MAUD *exits*)

EDDY (*Sits again*)   Yeah. Well, like I was saying . . . It may sound funny coming from a man who admits he wasn't much of a husband the first time out . . . but I swear to you, I think I could make a woman happy. The *right* woman.

ANN (*Trying to get in*)   Oh, I'm convi—

EDDY   I'd give her everything. She'd be a regular little queen. What I want above everything else is a family. My wife . . . my late wife . . . couldn't have children. I don't think a man's lived his life unless he leaves children. I'd like to have . . . (*Laughs*) Hell! I'll take as many as I can get!

ANN (*She also laughs, but nervously*)   I see.

EDDY   I'm only forty-five, and at forty-five a man is at his peak! And I just *know* I'll make a good husband for Trina.

ANN   Trina?

EDDY   Trina will make some little mother! That kid of yours.

ANN (*Stunned*)   Some little mother. Have you alerted Trina to this *project*?

EDDY   We love each other, Ann.

ANN (*Rises*)   I see.

EDDY   We want to get married right away. We don't see any point in waiting around.

ANN (*Politely*)   Certainly not with you at your peak. How long has this been going on?

EDDY (*Rises*)   Well, to tell you the truth . . . you may not like this but . . . ever since that first night . . . the night we all went out together. It happened just like that.

ANN   But you kept it secret? That wasn't very nice, Eddy.

EDDY   I know that. It's been about to drive me crazy. But Trina was so sure you . . . that you'd—

ANN   That I'd what?

EDDY   I've never been around girls Trina's age—I mean around them and their mothers—I didn't know what to believe. Trina was so sure you'd be . . . (*Forces himself*) *Jealous.* Hell! Trina thinks just because *she's* interested in me, every other woman is too. (*Chuckles*) She's such a kid.

ANN   Yes, she is. Too much of a kid for marriage.

EDDY   Why? The way I see it, a woman of eighteen . . .

ANN   Trina's only seventeen.

EDDY   (*Surprised*)   She *is?* (*Rather pleased*) Why the little devil. (*Laughs*) Well, the way I see it, a woman of . . . seventeen, eighteen . . . and a man of forty-five are a perfect balance.

ANN   Maybe in the Ozarks, Eddy. But not in this zip code.

EDDY   I love her, Ann.

ANN   Oh, for God's sake! If you're fool enough to let yourself fall in love with a *child* . . .
          (*She stops herself*)

EDDY   If I'm a fool, well, I'll just have to live with it.

ANN   Fine. And Trina will live with me.

EDDY   (*Goes to her*)   You're going to find Trina's made up her own mind about where she's going to live.

ANN   Eddy . . . how would you like ten to twenty in the state pen?

EDDY   (*Takes her shoulders*)   You've got a lot to think about, Ann. I'm going to run along.
          (*He starts for the door*)

ANN   Now wait a minute, Eddy!

74

EDDY (*Blandly going on. At the door*)   And, honey, you just bear in mind what good care I'll take of Trina. And of you too.

ANN   Of *me?*

EDDY   Naturally. I'm going to be your son-in-law.
(EDDY *goes*)

ANN (*Bawls out*)   Trina!
(TRINA *appears immediately, and goes to* ANN)

TRINA (*Quickly takes the offensive*)   I might as well tell you right now, Mummy, that if you pull something square like trying to keep me from seeing Eddy, I'll just talk him into taking me to Tahiti or some place out of your reach until I'm eighteen and then we'll be married anyway.

ANN (*Cutting in*)   You are playing Juliet to a fairly sedate Romeo.

TRINA (*Coolly*)   I shouldn't think you'd want me to answer that in kind, Mummy.

ANN (*Trying to stay calm*)   Trina, my big mistake was not sending you to a good, tough military school!

TRINA   I'm going to marry Eddy.

ANN   Do you love him?

TRINA   I think so.

ANN   You think so.

TRINA   He's crazy about me. He makes all the decisions. It's so easy to be with him. You thought Eddy was nice enough for *you,* didn't you?

ANN   I wasn't contemplating marrying Eddy.

75

TRINA *(Passionately)* You don't contemplate marrying *anybody*. You'd have let Eddy hang around just the way you let a kid like Peter. Just hang around. Only Eddy would never have asked you to marry him because you'd have brushed him off long before he got to the point. Because *he's* too *possible*. He's a darling man, and I decided I'd be damned if I'd let you waste *him*. So I swiped him.
(She flings herself down in a chair)

ANN *(Moves a few steps toward* TRINA, *then stops)* So you swiped him.

TRINA Right from under your nose, Mummy.

ANN *(Goes to* TRINA, *speaking gently)* That couldn't have been so hard, Trina. I mean you are very young and very lovely. Any mother who thinks of competing with her daughter has lost before she starts.

TRINA Oh, I don't know. There's Peter.

ANN Did you want Peter?

TRINA It wouldn't have mattered much if I had.

ANN If you had, then what?

TRINA Tough beans, that's what. (ANN *moves away*) Anyway *(Rises)* I don't want Peter, I want Eddy.

ANN *(Turns)* Why? Why *Eddy?*

TRINA I told you! He's great. He takes care of me.

ANN Trina, I've taken care of you.

TRINA I'm sorry, Mummy, but you just don't make it as a father image.

ANN *(Moves away)* Oh boy!

76

TRINA (*Goes to* ANN) Oh, forget it, Mummy. You've done okay.

ANN Oh, Trina, have I?
(*They embrace spontaneously*)

TRINA You let me run all over you, of course, but you're so sweet that whenever you *try* to stand up to me I make it a point to give in. (*Moves away*) If it's not too important.
(MAUD *risks a glance through the hallway*)

MAUD Is he gone? (*Not seeing* EDDY, *she comes into the room*) Well! What was *that* all about? I obviously walked in in the middle of *something.*

ANN What you walked in in the middle of was a proposal.

MAUD *Eddy?* Oh, Ann! (*Goes to* ANN, *and embraces her warmly, rocking her maternally*) Oh, my precious girl! I'm so happy for you!

ANN (*Gently disentangling herself*) Mother . . . it's not me Eddy wants to marry, Mother . . . it's Trina.

MAUD (*Disengages herself after a moment*) What? What in the world is *wrong* with everybody? Everyone's gone mad! Or is it *me?* (*Doing a complete about-face, she crosses to* TRINA) Trina! My darling girl! I'm so happy for you!

(*It is* TRINA *who now suffers* MAUD's *embrace. There is a blackout. Then rock-'n'-roll music is heard*)

The scene is ANN's *office, a few days later, around noon.*
MRS. MARGOLIN *and* BILLY *are onstage. She is sitting at the*
desk, typing. He is sitting in the chair in front of the desk.

BILLY   *Trina and Eddy.*

MRS. MARGOLIN *(Types the rhythm)*   They've-set-the-date.

BILLY   Little Trina and Big Ed. I can't believe it! *(Cheer-*
fully) At least he's still in the family. I think I'll enjoy
having a rich son-in-law.

MRS. MARGOLIN   Mr. Boylan!

BILLY   I take a European view of these things, Margy: *Honi*
soit qui mal y pense.

MRS. MARGOLIN   Huh?

BILLY   Never give a sucker an even break.
           (ANN *enters from her office, carrying a file which she*
           places on MRS. MARGOLIN's *desk)*

ANN   Here are the plans for the Gordonson place. *(Goes to*
BILLY) Hi, Billy. Glad you could make it.
           (*She puts her hands on his shoulders*)

BILLY   I've just heard the news from *(Pointing to* MRS.
MARGOLIN) Walter Cronkite here. Is that what you
wanted to see me about?

ANN   I just wanted to talk to you a bit.

MRS. MARGOLIN *(Being tactful)*   I think I'll have an early

lunch. (*Rises, gets her coat and bag, and starts for the door*) I'll be about an hour and a half, if you don't mind.
(*She looks at them*)

ANN It's all right.

MRS. MARGOLIN (*At the door*) I thought maybe I'd look for something to give the little bride. I may stop in at F.A.O. Schwarz.
(*She goes*)

BILLY How's the morale, little buddy? Not zonked?

ANN I'm not at all zonked!

BILLY That's the spirit.

ANN Oh, Billy . . . don't treat me as if I'd been left waiting at the altar. The big Eddy romance was all in *your* mind, and Mrs. Margolin's, and Maud's. *I* was never interested in Eddy! I was just helping him out.

BILLY Well, now he's got Trina to help him.

ANN But who's going to help Trina?

BILLY Haven't you noticed yet that Trina helps herself? Look, this is the best thing that could have happened to Trina. *And* you. I think Trina was right on the edge of giving you a hard time. You have lucked out.

ANN Billy! He's *twenty-eight* years older than she is! It's grotesque!

BILLY Why?

ANN (*Curiously*) You don't think it is?

BILLY No. He's a very lively fellow; Trina's quite mature in many ways . . . It's a perfectly natural attraction. (*Rises, and walks a few steps*) Actually, Ann, you'd be

79

surprised how devastating younger girls find *me*. There's
something very sexy about this age . . .

ANN (*Almost to herself*)   Have you noticed that, too?

BILLY (*Stops*)   Too?

ANN (*Sits down at the desk*)   What if *I* told *you* that I've
had a proposal?

BILLY (*Riveted*)   *You? No!* Who?

ANN   Me! Yes! Peter Latham *who!*

BILLY   Peter Latham! You mean that *kid? Trina's* little boyfriend?

ANN   He's not Trina's little boyfriend. He's *my* little boyfriend.

BILLY   And he's asked *you* to marry him? (*Leans against the
file, and howls with laughter. Then goes back to the desk*)
What's he on? You've got to keep your eyes open with
kids that age.

ANN   I'm so grateful for your solicitude, Billy dear. But I've
known Peter for quite some time. He is not on drugs. He
is extremely intelligent, holds down a responsible position
in the family business—Hohenhauser *Steel,* that is.

BILLY   Well, sure. But . . .

ANN (*Going on*)   He has money of his own, a mind of his
own and he wants to marry *me*. Raddled, old broken-
down, liver-spotty *me!* He's even met you and Maud and
he *still* wants to marry me.

(BILLY *stares open-mouthed for a long moment*)

BILLY   He must have a thing about his mother. Has he
talked much about his mother?

ANN   He says she's very like Trina.

BILLY   Annie! You don't mean you're taking this seriously! He's a baby! A little, bitty baby!
(He is holding his hand about a foot from the floor)

ANN   He's twenty-two. Were you a baby at twenty-two?

BILLY   You're damn right I was. A little, bitty baby!
(He repeats the hand gesture)

ANN   Well, he isn't.

BILLY *(Peers at her)*   Are you *serious?* I can't believe it!

ANN *(Grimly)*   Believe it.

BILLY   But, Jesus, honey! Have you thought . . .

ANN   What people would say?

BILLY   Yes.

ANN *(She rises, and pretends she's entering a café with* PETER*)*   If *you* saw us, and you didn't know us, if you saw Peter and me together in some public place, what would you think?
(She moves slightly apart from the imaginary PETER*)*

BILLY *(Looking at the "couple"—first one, then the other)*   I'd think you were shelling out.

ANN   Do I look . . . like the kind of woman who "shells out"?

BILLY   No, of course you don't, Annie. I didn't mean that.

ANN *(Plaintively)*   I don't think we look too utterly ridiculous together. I check mirrors constantly, I mean, if we go anywhere. People don't *stare* at us, Billy. I don't know if you are aware of it, but the latest statistics prove that a woman comes into her full sexual flowering at forty, while a man attains his at twenty.

81

BILLY   So you're in full flower, eh, kid? (*Reaching for her*) Give us a whiff—
   (ANN *angrily pushes him away*)

ANN   Damn it, I'm serious.

BILLY (*Stares at her a moment, then turns away, quietly angry*) Okay. If the kid is to your taste—what the hell. Youth is great. Enjoy. (*Takes out a cigar*) We won't talk about it any more.

ANN (*Goes to him*)   You don't get it. It's not his *youth* that's to my taste. It bothers me terribly. But he's really a marvelous person. He's quite extraordinary. Very strong-*minded*. And he has a good deal of money. Once I stopped to think about it . . . the overall picture, you understand . . . it suddenly seemed—rather marvelous. I'd given up thinking about . . . well, actually, I guess I had kind of put myself out to pasture. And suddenly, here is this hand-some, intelligent, *rich, young* man who thinks that *I* am the *greatest*. Billy, he loves me. He could have anybody he wants, and he wants *me*.

BILLY (*Really for the first time believing her, he speaks quietly*)   Well—wow.

ANN   Peter wants to *marry* me. Take care of me. It's the damnedest thing. But after all these years, after two marriages, I finally find someone strong who (*Realizes what she has said*) I'm sorry, Billy.

BILLY   That's okay. Say it like it is.

ANN   I finally found someone strong who really takes over. And he's a twenty-two-year-old boy.

BILLY (*Opens the top drawer of the file, and leans on it*) Annushka, you're in *love* with the kid.

ANN (*Sits on the bench*) Oh, for heaven's sake, Billy. I'm forty years old! It's quite enough to *be* loved. And have a few of my tomorrows taken care of.

BILLY I see. It's to be a union of love on his part and fatigue on yours. Is that correct?

ANN I don't want to talk about it any more. Let's go have lunch.
(*She rises*)

BILLY (*Slams the file drawer shut*) You'll have to forgive me, darling. I seem to have lost my appetite. I'll call you tomorrow.

ANN All right, tomorrow. (*He starts away, indicating a baby's height again*) You're angry.

BILLY (*Shouts*) I'm not angry. I'm *never* angry!
(*He goes.* ANN *reflects a moment, then she moves to the phone with a resolute air, and dials*)

ANN Hello ... Hello, is that you, Peter? ... Well this is me. And I called to say that, after thinking it over carefully, weighing everything, pro and con, I've decided that— Peter, don't interrupt me! . . . Well, *okay!* (*She, too, shouts angrily*) The answer's *okay!*

(*There is a blackout. Then Greek music is heard*)

SCENE THREE

It is three weeks later in ANN's *apartment.* ANN *is offstage in the bedroom.* PETER *is standing near the bedroom door.*

PETER But, Ann . . .

ANN (*Offstage*) I *can't!* I *won't!*

PETER Ann . . .

ANN (*Entering from the bedroom, and crossing to the mirror*) You can't expect me to! Look at my hair! I *do not want to meet them.*

PETER Why are you carrying on like this?

ANN (*Frantically looking for a cigarette*) Because you've given me absolutely no warning. Look at my hair.

PETER (*Going to her*) If I'd given you any more warning, you'd have wriggled out of it.

ANN (*Takes a cigarette from the coffee table*) Couldn't it *please* wait until we get back?

PETER (*Takes the cigarette from her*) I want them to meet you before we get married. Look, it's better this way— more spontaneous. When Mother called this morning and said they were stopping off on their way to Paris, I thought, *now.* Let's get it over with. So I told them.

ANN So you told them! My God! What a scene that must have . . .

PETER I've told you twenty times what their reaction was.

84

They were just . . . (*Lamely*) surprised. That's all. Surprised.

ANN Oh, Peter.

PETER It had to happen sooner or later.

ANN What's wrong with later? We could have stalled a little (*Eagerly*) They could have come to my *funeral*. (*Goes toward him*) Look, I would have liked some time to prepare myself for this . . . this interview.

PETER It is not an *interview*. You're not applying for a position as an upstairs maid.

ANN They despise me.

PETER (*He embraces her*) How can they despise you? They haven't met you.

ANN (*A beat, then her hand goes to her stomach*) Peter, I don't feel at all well. (*Moves to the sofa, and sits*) And look at my *hair!*

PETER Stop it! You know perfectly well that nothing depends on this visit. We're going to be married next week no matter what. If this meeting goes down moderately well, everything will be a hell of a lot easier, that's all. And if they don't like it (*He grins*) screw 'em.

ANN (*Hollowly*) Screw 'em.

PETER I'll be interested to see how you react to the old man. He's something on wheels. Self-made, you know.

ANN I thought he married . . . I mean, your mother is a Hohenhauser . . .

PETER Oh, that's not the way my father went about it. He grabbed the company away from my grandfather, kicked

85

the old boy into astonished retirement, *then* took over the daughter. Along with everything else in sight.

ANN   My goodness! Your poor old grandfather.

PETER   Ha! My "poor old grandfather" just met his match, that's all. Used to bash his way through picket lines with a seven iron. He liked to show it to me. Eight notches on it. *Still* . . . my father took the old boy on and whipped his ears off and set himself up there as king of the hill before he was thirty-five. (*Grins*) Want to know something? He's next.

ANN (*Astonished*)   You're just a kid.

PETER (*Steps toward her*)   Shall I tell you why Dad will be willing to go along with my marrying you? Because he thinks you'll distract *me*. He knows *his* turn is coming up. He feels me breathing down his neck and he's not ready for the axe.

ANN (*Rather alarmed*)   Oh, Peter, that's . . .

PETER   Don't worry. I'm giving him five more years. (*Coolly*) He's five years from retirement. (*The doorbell rings.* ANN *jumps up, giving a little yelp.* PETER *kisses her briefly, and starts for the door. He turns to give her an encouraging look*) It's okay, lady. You're with me. *Fix your hair!* (*He grins teasingly at* ANN, *then opens the door.* MR. *and* MRS. LATHAM *enter.* MRS. LATHAM *is very trim with a youthful bearing. She is extremely elegant; she wears the best of everything. Very lacquered, in quiet, deadly professional good taste*) Well, here you are . . . (*Token kiss*) Mother.

MRS. LATHAM   Darling. . .

PETER   Come in, Dad.
   (MRS. LATHAM *moves across the room, looking*

around. MR. LATHAM *hands* ANN *his hat without looking at her, as though she were the maid. She places the hat on the table)*

MRS. LATHAM   Darling, can you believe the coincidence? It's weird. Weird, weird, weird. Aunt Phillis and I spent two winters in New York right after I came out, and I used to take voice lessons from a Madame Somebody *right here in this very building!* Right here in . . .

PETER   Mother, I want you to meet Ann. (MRS. LATHAM *turns with a bright smile to* ANN, *and crosses to her, hand outstretched.* PETER *moves toward* ANN) This is my father, Ann. Mother, this is Ann.

MRS. LATHAM (*Crossing to* ANN)   Ah, Miss Stanley . . . Mrs. . . .

ANN   Mrs.

MRS. LATHAM (*Pleasantly*)   Mrs. Stanley . . . I'm delighted to meet you.
      (*They shake hands.* MR. LATHAM *bows*)

ANN   I . . . I'm so glad you were able to come.

MR. LATHAM (*Bluntly*)   Peter insisted.

ANN   Yes. Yes, I know he did. (*A moment's silence*) Please sit down. (MR. LATHAM *sits on the sofa*) Let me fix you a drink.

PETER (*To* ANN)   Let me do it, Ann. I know what they like.
      (*He walks over to the bar*)

MRS. LATHAM (*Moving around the room*)   What a charming apartment. Sweet . . . and you've decorated it so . . . *bravely.* Sweet, sweet, sweet! Edgar?
      (*Gives* MR. LATHAM *a look*)

MR. LATHAM   Sweet.

MRS. LATHAM (*Picking up a small framed snapshot of* ANN *from the desk*)   And what a pretty picture of you.

ANN   It's . . . quite an old one . . .

MRS. LATHAM   I used to wear my hair exactly the same way! Remember, Edgar?
(*She hands him the picture*)

MR. LATHAM (*He looks at it, then gives it back*)   No.

MRS. LATHAM   Oh, of course you do. I was carrying Peter then . . .
(*She goes to* PETER *at the bar*)

PETER (*Firmly takes the picture from her, and puts it on the desk again, and hands her a drink*)   Mother.
(*She takes the drink, and looks momentarily distressed as she realizes she has made a faux pas*)

MR. LATHAM   Don't fix anything for me, Peter. We haven't enough time.

MRS. LATHAM (*Returning to the sofa*)   Oh Lord. With Edgar it's always rush, rush, rush.

MR. LATHAM (*It's obvious that he has decided to speak. He rises, and steps forward, hands in pockets*)   Mrs. Stanley. Actually, I'm glad to have this opportunity to—uh—

ANN (*Charmingly*)   Size me up.

MR. LATHAM (*Laughs easily*)   Yes. I didn't know what to expect. (*Steps closer to her*) All things considered, I'm very agreeably surprised.

ANN   I'm glad.

MR. LATHAM (*He looks at* PETER, *then turns back*)   Tell me, why are you marrying him?

ANN   I . . . (*Hesitates*) I think what you want to know is why Peter is marrying me.

MR. LATHAM   Well?

ANN   I know what he tells me.

MR. LATHAM   And what is that?

ANN (*Gathers herself*)   That he loves me and if you don't like it . . . you can . . .
> (*She stops short, realizing what she has almost said*)

MR. LATHAM (*Turns to his wife accusingly*)   He's a real Hohenhauser. Just like your father! (*Turns back to* ANN) You know that he's only twenty-two.

ANN   I know.

MR. LATHAM   He just voted for the first time (*Looks at* PETER)—and *wrong.* (ANN *smiles.* MR. LATHAM *turns back to her*) You realize, don't you, that you'll eventually have to live in Pittsburgh. You won't like Pittsburgh.

ANN   I haven't thought much about that.

MR. LATHAM   You'll *have* to think about it when I retire . . . and Peter takes over the company.

ANN (*A beat*)   But, I won't have to face that for a very long time, will I?
> (*She exchanges a look with* PETER)

PETER (*Grins*)   Dad, you're just going to make a fool of yourself.

MR. LATHAM (*Amiably*)   Well, son, I can afford to make a fool of myself. (*To* ANN) I can afford *almost anything.* (ANN *smiles apprehensively. He goes on casually, with a smile*) Of course, you're not interested in the subject of money . . .
> (*He turns his back to her*)

ANN Oh, yes, I am.

MR. LATHAM (*Turns to her, and laughs*) Ah, well, in that case . . .

PETER (*Warning*) Dad . . .

MR. LATHAM I can easily top anything you might expect from Peter—

PETER *Dad* . . .

MR. LATHAM . . . and we can all shake hands.

PETER How about me, Dad? Who do *I* shake hands with?

MR. LATHAM With yourself, son. You shake hands with yourself.

ANN (*Firmly*) Mr. Latham . . .

MR. LATHAM (*Turning back to her*) Yes, Mrs. Stanley?

ANN I know the value of money. I wouldn't marry Peter if he didn't have some. But I'm not marrying him *for* his money. And I'm not throwing him over for *yours*.
(*They lock stares*)

MR. LATHAM (*Shrugs, and gives her a small bow*) Mrs. Stanley.

ANN Mr. Latham.

MR. LATHAM (*Starting up to the door*) Christine.

MRS. LATHAM (*Small mocking bow*) Edgar.

MR. LATHAM Come along.

MRS. LATHAM But I'm not going with you, Edgar. (*He stops*) I *told* you. I'm going to meet Cynthia. (*He makes an impatient sound. She looks at her watch*) And I'm a few minutes early. I'll stay on and finish this.

PETER (*Moving toward the door, puts his arm around his father's shoulder*) Come on, Dad . . . I'll buy you a drink. You need it.
> (*He goes, giving* ANN *a wink and the thumb and forefinger circle of "well done"*)

MR. LATHAM (*To* MRS. LATHAM) Your father! Just like your goddam father!
> (*He goes, closing the door.* ANN *and* MRS. LATHAM *are left alone. They smile tentatively*)

MRS. LATHAM Actually, *he's* the one who's like my goddam father. Absolute bastards, both of them.

ANN And Peter?

MRS. LATHAM Peter's a darling. Willful, of course, but a darling. Always was. (*Smiles, pats the sofa, inviting* ANN *to sit by her;* ANN *does so*) I shall miss him very much. Boys seem to just *go away* when they grow up. He was always marvelous company. When he was little, he used to say, "When I grow up, I'm going to marry my mummy!"
> (*Face to face, for a moment; then* MRS. LATHAM *turns away, realizing her gaff*)

ANN (*Rises*) Well, there you are. I'm a dream come true!

MRS. LATHAM It's a curse! Every time I open my mouth!
> (*She rises, and goes to the bar to fix a drink*)

ANN (*Sighs*) It's the situation. It will take getting used to. (*Indicating* MRS. LATHAM's *drink*) Let me.

MRS. LATHAM (*Waves her off, goes to bar*) I'm going to call you Ann.

ANN Of course.

MRS. LATHAM And I'm Christine. You know, I find myself liking you very much. Do you golf?

ANN   I'm afraid not.

MRS. LATHAM (*Cheerfully. Sits in a chair*)   Oh, well. We
can always shop. Shop, shop, shop! (*Gives* ANN *a long,
speculative look*) My hunch is you'll make Peter very
happy.

ANN (*Sits on an arm of the sofa*)   Do you really think so?

MRS. LATHAM   Why shouldn't you? Youth in a woman is
frightfully overrated. Look at me. When I was young, I
was homely and self-conscious and shy, shy, shy! Actually,
I was incapable of thinking of anything or anyone but
myself. Mercifully, one grows up. One's responses to life
at forty are infinitely more *tender*. Tender, tender, tender!
Don't you see? You are at the very height of your . . .

ANN (*Drily*)   Full sexual flowering?

MRS. LATHAM   I *like* that! (*Rises, crosses to the sofa and
sits*) Shall I tell you what I really think? I think you are
lucky, and I think Peter's lucky. Take me. Stuck with
Edgar. Edgar, Edgar . . . (*Takes a drink*) Oh, well. There's
always golf. (*Perks up a bit*) One must simply organize
one's life *around* the Edgars. (*Looks at her watch*) A
quarter to already! It's not possible! I must run.
        (*She rises, and puts her glass on the bar. The door-
        bell rings*)

ANN (*Starts for the door*)   Excuse me . . .
        (*She goes to the door and opens it. A handsome young
        man appears, very fashionably turned out. He is
        PATRICK GRAHAM*) Yes?

PAT   Hello.

MRS. LATHAM   Pat! Now really!

PAT (*Goes to her*)   Christine, I've been waiting fifteen

minutes. That's my *outside* limit. One could starve, starve, starve.

MRS. LATHAM (*Laughs*)   Oh, you are spoiled.

PAT   I saw the old boy pull out, and I thought I'd come up. (*Smiles with charming intimacy at* ANN, *and goes to her*) She gets to talking and loses all sense of time.

MRS. LATHAM (*Goes to them*)   Ann dear, I'd like to present Patrick Graham.

PAT (*Another radiant smile*)   Hello, Ann.
       (*They shake hands*)

ANN   How do you do?

MRS. LATHAM   Patrick is one of our most promising young golfers. He was second at Pinehurst last year. I can't tell you how thrilling it was!

PAT (*Charming pout*)   But she's sending me off alone to the big Phoenix open. All by myself. (*Smiles shyly, sexily, at* ANN) Tell her she shouldn't do that.

MRS. LATHAM (*To* PAT)   Don't bother, pet. (*Touches his arm*) You can't win 'em all. She's already booked. Booked, booked, booked. (*Pushes him up toward the door. Turns tranquilly to* ANN, *smiles, and holds out her arms*) Good-bye, Ann.
       (*They brush cheeks. She goes to the door*)

ANN   Goodbye.

MRS. LATHAM   I'm so glad we've met.

PAT   Goodbye.

MRS. LATHAM (*Looks at* PAT, *turns back to* ANN, *and smiles serenely*)   Welcome to the family.

       (*There is a blackout. Then fast gypsy music is heard*)

The scene is ANN's *apartment, a week later.* MAUD *enters from the kitchen, dressed in country tweeds. She is carrying a pot of poinsettias. She puts them on the card table, moving the ferns on the card table to the bookcase upstage of the sofa.* BILLY *is at the bar, mixing a drink.*

BILLY   Maud, will you stop moving Birnam Woods and give it to me straight?

MAUD   They're *flying* to *Mexico tomorrow. Peter's* idea. They plan to be married on Christmas Eve. *Christmas Eve!* It's sacrilegious! I wash my hands of the whole affair. (*Sits down angrily on the sofa*) I've done more than my share trying to fight this lunacy. Trina hasn't turned a hand, and she won't let Eddy open his mouth.

BILLY   I don't know what the hell would have been solved by letting Eddy run around with his mouth open.
       (*He starts to sit next to her on the sofa*)

MAUD   And as for *you.* Nobody's ever been able to count on you. (*Under this attack,* BILLY *gets up, goes to a chair, and sits*) I should have known you'd pick a time like this to disappear . . .

BILLY   I got called to the Coast. Besides, I think maybe it's better for me to stay outside it for the time being.

MAUD   That's right. The passive line has always been *your* great technique. Poor Ann.

94

BILLY   Maud, you haven't been my mother-in-law for a long time. How would you like a boot in the tail?

MAUD   Snarling at me isn't going to help Ann. Or *me*. Can you imagine how *I* feel? Having that nasty little boy for a son-in-law! You should see him jumping around Ann . . . devouring her with his eyes . . . It's gruesome. The boy's not normal. Thank God he didn't get his hands on Trina!

BILLY   How *about* Trina?

MAUD   Eddy is a perfect love! They're *marvelous* together. Trina just leads him around by the nose. (*The doorbell rings*) There! I guess you know who *that* is! If you don't mind, Billy, *you* can let him in.
   (*She rises, and starts for the hall*)

BILLY   Where do you think you're going?

MAUD   To finish my packing. Trina and Eddy are taking me to the country. I shall spend Christmas as I should. With my grandchildren.
   (*She exits. The doorbell rings again.* BILLY *opens the door. It is* PETER)

BILLY   Well, hello young Peter!
   (BILLY *closes the door.* PETER's *cool through the following scene is exemplary. At* BILLY's *opening thrust,* PETER *reacts with controlled good humor*)

PETER   Hello, old man. When did you get back?

BILLY   Glad to see me?

PETER   Ann was complaining that you'd deserted us.

BILLY   Never! I dashed back the minute my little job was finished. Well. How about offering me a drink?

PETER (*Gives* BILLY *a curious look, but goes to the bar, and starts mixing a drink*)   All tuckered out?

95

BILLY   Not particularly, why?
(*He sits*)

PETER (*Shrugs and indicates the bar, where he has put himself at* BILLY'*s service*)   Oh . . . you're pretty much at home around here.

BILLY (*Smiles charmingly, indicates* PETER *himself*)   New management.

PETER   Scotch?

BILLY   Please. (PETER *pours*) With a splash of soda. (PETER *nods, takes up a bottle, but can't find an opener*) What's the problem?

PETER   The bottle opener seems to have disappeared.

BILLY   There's an extra one that's kept in the black lacquer box on the left of the ice bucket.

PETER (*Opens the box, finds the opener*)   Thanks. I'll make a note of it.
(*He holds it up triumphantly for* BILLY *to see. They smile a good scout's smile at each other*)

BILLY   Good boy. You're a lucky guy.

PETER   Yes, I am.
(PETER *takes a drink for himself, and hands* BILLY *his*)

BILLY   Oh, thank you. (*Raises the glass*) Here's to love. (*They start to clink glasses and miss. They drink*) Is Ann going to give up the business?

PETER   We haven't really talked about it.
(*He sits*)

BILLY   Now that she's got somebody to take care of her. That is . . . (*Manages without words to convey the idea that* ANN *knows a good financial thing when she sees it*) *really* take care of her. If you know what I mean.

PETER (*Pleasantly*) Yeah. I know what you mean.

BILLY (*Drinks quietly, then tries another flank*) I hear you're going to be married in Mexico.

PETER That's right.

BILLY But with no family . . . no friends around? I'd hoped to be part of the wedding party.

PETER Really?

BILLY Yes.

PETER Now where did I get the impression that you were very anti the whole thing?

BILLY I can't imagine.

PETER Then you aren't?

BILLY (*Leans forward*) Does it matter to you?

PETER (*Leans in a bit*) Not to *me,* no. But Ann is very fond of you.

BILLY (*After a beat*) You're not a bad kid.

PETER So what is it you can't swallow?

BILLY (*Shrugs*) Appearances, I guess.

PETER (*Quietly*) Appearances.

BILLY Next to Ann—now don't get me wrong, fella— but next to Ann, you don't appear to be . . . completely . . . mature . . .

PETER (*Smiles*) Whereas you do. Shows you how appearances can be deceiving.

97

(BILLY *slowly, ominously rises.* PETER *rises to face him. They stare at each other for a moment.* ANN *comes out of her room. Her hair and dress are more youthful than we have seen them before*)

ANN (*Goes to* BILLY. *They embrace*)   Billy! Why didn't someone tell me you were here? Oh, I'm so glad you got back! Did Peter tell you we're leaving tomorrow?
(*She holds* BILLY'S *hand, then takes* PETER'S *hand.* BILLY *looks at her*)

BILLY   Yes. He told me. You look . . . well, wowareenie!

ANN   I'm switched on for the Electric Circus.

BILLY   New hairdo.

ANN   Kenneth. Peter says any woman who can't spend a hundred dollars a week on her hair and face and fingertips isn't *trying.*

BILLY   Is *that* what Peter says?

PETER   Uh huh.

ANN   Do you like?

BILLY   I like. (*A gentle smile*) I always liked.
(*He pulls* ANN *to him. She pulls her hand away*)

ANN (*Glorying in this tacit rivalry between the two men*) Ah! *Now* you tell me. Well, it's too late. I am (*Smiles tenderly at* PETER) bespoke. (*Turns back to* BILLY *with a look of happy malice*) Oh, say, I saw Elke Schnitzel in the elevator yesterday. *Her* nose was running.

BILLY   Now, don't knock my bit of holiday cheer. Her boss is leaving, and Elke and I have the place to ourselves. But enough of me. Where are you headed in that extravaganza?

ANN   We're going to Max's Kansas City for dinner, then to
Café La Mama, then to the Electric Circus. Then, maybe
later to the Graffiti. Who knows? The night's before us.

BILLY *(To* ANN*)*   How things have changed! *(To* PETER*)*
I can't ever remember being able to keep Ann out past
eleven-thirty.

ANN   Well, now I love it! Don't I, Peter?

PETER   She loves it.

BILLY   She loves it. *(Crosses to the sofa, hitting the side of
his head, and sits)* I went to the Electric Circus once.
Just *once.*

ANN   If you think I'm going to be scared off by a little noise!
Hey, Billy! Wait till you see us zooming around town on
the new Triumph Trophy Two-Five-Oh!

BILLY   The new what?

PETER   It's a bike.

ANN   A *motorcycle.* Peter just bought it. *(Proudly)* We got
arrested last week! Oh, Billy, it was wild! *(Sits on an arm
of the sofa, à la motorcycle)* We were pulled up waiting
for a light at Third and Seventieth, and this black leather-
jacket va-va-varoomed up beside us and said, "Whaddaya
get outa the tricycle, Louise?" "Lew-eeze!" He couldn't
have been more offensive! So I said, "If you can get somebody to help you tow that junk heap over to the Drive,
we'll see who can get what!" So he gunned after us
(Makes motorcycle noise) and we got on the Drive and he
never came close to us! Unfortunately, at Ninety-Sixth
Street there was this cop. *(Makes motorcycle noise) He*
came close to us.
   *(*ANN *and* PETER *laugh)*

BILLY (*A long beat as he regards her, then he turns quietly to* PETER) Another Scotch. Deep dish.

PETER Yes, sir.
(*He takes his glass, and goes to the bar.* TRINA *opens the front door; she and* EDDY *appear*)

TRINA Hi.

EDDY Hi, everybody.

ANN Hi.
(MAUD *surges into the room from the hall, ready to leave, an overnight bag in hand*)

MAUD You didn't have to come up, darlings. I could easily have met you downstairs.

TRINA (*Goes to* ANN, *followed by* EDDY) I wanted to see Mummy before she leaves.
(ANN *goes to meet her. They embrace*)

ANN Hello, darling. (*Goes to* EDDY) Hello, Eddy.

EDDY (*Hesitates a moment, then starts to shake her hand*) Mother.
(*He chuckles, then kisses her on the cheek*)

ANN Have you time for a drink?

EDDY I think maybe we'd better not—the roads are going to be crowded as hell.

ANN Oh, dear, I always hate it when I know Trina is out in holiday traffic . . .

BILLY At least *Trina* is in a *car*.
(*He makes motorcycle noise*)

TRINA Oh, Mummy, may I have a word with you?

ANN   Will you excuse us?
(*She follows* TRINA *into her bedroom*)

MAUD (*To* EDDY)   I want to stop and pick up some tree ornaments. There never are enough . . .

EDDY (*Goes to the bar*)   Okay. You may be right. I thought I'd about bought out the store, but that tree's ten feet tall. (*To* BILLY) I told them to send the biggest one they had.
(BILLY *smiles*)

MAUD   If only it will snow. We can go to midnight Mass at the little church in the village. (*To* BILLY) Eddy got truffles for the turkey dressing.

PETER (*Grins*)   Truffles!

EDDY (*Goes to* PETER)   It's a twenty-pounder! I told them to get the biggest one they had. (*Turns to* BILLY) Who're you spending Christmas with, Billy boy?

BILLY   As luck would have it, I'm having Christmas right here in the building. I'm sharing my loneliness with another single.

EDDY (*To* PETER)   I'll bet it's a big blond single.

BILLY   I told them to get the biggest one they had!
(*They laugh*)

MAUD   You're going to be here in the building? Then would you do me a little favor, Billy dear? Would you be kind enough to stop in and water my ferns?

BILLY   Ferns?

MAUD (*Hands a key to* BILLY)   I was madly worried about the ferns. Now not too much water.

BILLY   Just a splash. (*Indicating his drink*) The way I take it. (*To* EDDY) Say, Ed, when is the big day for you and Trina?

EDDY   I wanted Trina to finish high school . . . (*Hesitates*) But . . . uh . . . (*Laughs*) She doesn't want to wait. So I guess we're gonna get the job done pretty soon.

MAUD (*Firmly*)   Not until the clothes we've ordered are ready. I insisted that Trina have a proper trousseau.

EDDY   So I've got to wait for word from Paraphernalia, whatever the hell *that* is.
      (ANN *and* TRINA *return*)

TRINA   Are you ready, Granny Maud?

EDDY (*Grabbing her bag and going to the door*)   We're off, folks!

TRINA   Goodbye, Mummy. I hope you'll be happy. I really do.

ANN (*We see that she is moved*)   Oh, Trina!
      (*She kisses her*)

TRINA (*Goes to* BILLY)   Merry Christmas, Billy. (*Kisses* BILLY, *then turns to* PETER) You'd better be good to my mother.
      (*She goes to the door*)

EDDY   All the best, Ann.

ANN   To you too, Eddy.

MAUD (*Going to* BILLY)   Joyeux Noël, Billy dear. (*Gives him a peck. Goes to* ANN) Merry Christmas, Ann.
      (*They kiss*)

ANN   Merry Christmas, Mother.

MAUD (*Passes* PETER *on her way to the door and shakes her head disparagingly*) Hohenhauser!
(*She goes, followed by* TRINA *and* EDDY)

BILLY (*Gets up*) Well, I guess I'll follow the general movement . . .

ANN No. Stay. Please.

BILLY What's the matter?

ANN Trina is pregnant.

BILLY Oh? (*To* PETER) Now she'll never finish high school. (*To* ANN) Is she terribly upset?

ANN She? *Me!*

PETER Forget it, Ann.

ANN Forget it? She's only seventeen. And she's my daughter. My only child. And I'm . . . (*A thought*) Oh, I'm going to be a grandmother!

BILLY (*To* PETER) I guess we know what that makes you. (*Hands him a cigar*) Have a cigar.

PETER Come on, Ann. We were going out, so let's go out.

ANN Poor little Trina.

PETER Poor little Trina! She could have kept the big news until after our wedding.

ANN Oh, Peter . . .

BILLY I'm forced to agree with young Peter.

ANN (*Gives a shaky little laugh*) You've got to admit my cup runneth over.

BILLY   You're the sexiest grandmother in my crowd.

ANN   Thank you for being here tonight, Billy.

BILLY   Oh, I'm *always* here. Don't you know that? You know, I've just figured out what it is that's been bugging me all evening . . . I'm jealous.
    (*He goes*)

PETER (*When* BILLY *is gone*)   He meant it, you know, what he said. He *is* jealous. And he's surprised that he is.

ANN   He's just that perverse! He was never jealous when we were married.

PETER   I am . . . extremely jealous of him. I feel very threatened by Billy.

ANN   Well, you needn't. You're terribly possessive, you know.

PETER   I know. Every time I see you even shake hands with another guy, I get a big blast of the old territorial imperative.

ANN   I can never believe it will last . . .

PETER   It will last as long as you want it. I'll be here as long as you'll have me.

ANN   *Why?*

PETER (*Grins*)   Because you're very neat with Kleenex.

ANN   Peter. I do wish I'd known you sooner.
    (*They embrace*)

PETER   I like now.

ANN   Oh, I like now, too. Do you know that for the first time

in my life I can really *count* on someone else? (*Wryly*)
And a little child shall lead her . . .

PETER   Ann, I swear to God, if you make one more joke
about my age . . .

ANN   Shut up. I'm older than you!
   (*She kisses him*)

PETER   Let's skip the Electric Circus.
   (*He embraces her*)

ANN   Not on your life! I'm already plugged in.

   (*She does a dance step. There is a blackout. Then
   rock-'n'-roll music is heard, and strobes start flashing*)

The scene is ANN's *apartment. It is the same evening, around midnight. After a moment, the front door opens.* ANN *and* PETER *enter. He turns on the lights. She removes her coat and tosses it on a chair.*

ANN   Oh my God! How can you stand it!

PETER   It's just a joint. It's okay.

ANN   *Okay?* It's an *assault!* That kind of bombardment could break down your chromosomes! How can you take it?
 (*She goes into the kitchen*)

PETER   It's just a joint!

ANN (*Comes out of the kitchen with a bottle of Alka Seltzer, and goes to the bar*)   You knew everybody in there! Every single solitary living whatever-they-were! Who was that girl dressed in Saran Wrap?
 (*She picks up a glass of water at the bar, and puts three Alka Seltzer tablets in it*)

PETER   Polly.

ANN   Oh. Polly. And that gloomy Botticelli who sat on you for half the evening? I failed to catch her name. If it was offered.

PETER   Gabriella . . . she's a nice kid . . . a little kinkie . . . but nice.

ANN   You seemed to know her well.

PETER   Sure, I know her.

ANN   Is there something between you?

PETER   No.

ANN   Never?

PETER   Not really.

ANN   But you've slept with her?

PETER   A couple of times.

ANN (*Puts in a fourth Alka Seltzer tablet*)   She's the most beautiful girl I've ever seen.

PETER (*Indifferently*)   Yeah, she's a beauty, all right.

ANN   What's the matter with you? She's breathtaking! How old is she? Eighteen? And you let something like that get away from you?

PETER (*Rises; speaks gently*)   What's the matter, Ann?

ANN   Nothing! It's just that that place got on my nerves. The environment was so animated and the inhabitants so inert!
    (*She slumps on the sofa*)

PETER   That's their style.

ANN   I daresay. (*Sighs*) I'm sorry, Peter. It was all a big mistake. We should have gone to . . . Radio City and Rumpelmayer's.

PETER   We'll be out of here tomorrow afternoon. Relax.
    (*He sits next to her*)

ANN   And thank goodness I've finished packing. I have a fantastically aching head.
    (*She leans back on his arm*)

PETER   Come on. Relax a little.

ANN   No . . . it's late. I'd rather you went on home, Peter. I'm absolutely done in. (*Rises; moves away*) I'll just finish this Alka Seltzer and go to bed.

PETER (*Following her*)   All right.

ANN   Don't be angry with me, Peter.

PETER   I'm not. But if I don't go right now, I won't go at all. Okay?
   (*He gives her a tender but brief kiss*)

ANN   Thank you, darling.

PETER (*Going to the door*)   I'll pick you up around eleven-thirty.

ANN   I'll be waiting.

PETER   Get some sleep now.

ANN   Oh, God, I just remembered. Mother snatched my last sleeping pill.

PETER   You sure you . . .

ANN   Oh, well, maybe the Alka Seltzer will do it.

PETER   Sure you don't want me to stay? I'll massage your neck . . . you're all tensed up . . .

ANN   I just want to crawl into bed and black out.

PETER (*A beat*)   Okay. Eleven-thirty.

ANN   Eleven-thirty.
   (*He goes.* ANN *goes to the bar, picks up the bottle of Alka Seltzer, sips from her glass, starts for her room, picking up her jacket and purse, and putting out the light. She is groaning with fatigue. The bedroom*

door opens and BILLY *appears. She backs into the living room. He is in his shirt-sleeves, with tie off, and drink and cigar in hand)*

BILLY (*Hoarse whisper*)   It's the Ghost of Christmas Past. (*He goes past her)*

ANN (*At the bedroom door*)   What are you doing here? Who let you in?

BILLY (*Same whisper*)   Maud gave me her key. To take care of the ferns.

ANN   Humbug! They don't need taking care of at this hour. They need their sleep.

BILLY (*Turns*)   Elke's still busy. And I knew you weren't here, so I just dropped in to look at your TV. When Elke finishes . . .

ANN   The TV is in *here*. What the devil are you doing in my bedroom?

BILLY   I ducked out when I heard you coming. I didn't want to compromise you.

ANN (*Furious*)   You've been standing behind that door with your fat ear pasted to the keyhole!

BILLY   It was hardly necessary. (*A beat*) If I were you, Ann, I wouldn't torture myself going on and on and on about all the pretty girls Peter . . .

ANN   Oh, stop it, Billy. Finish your drink. And fix me one. (*She turns the lights back on)*

BILLY   I thought you wanted me to go. (*She goes into the bedroom)*

ANN (*Offstage*)   Fix me a drink.

(*He goes to the bar. She leaves the door open while* BILLY *fixes her drink and refills his own. He raises his voice so she can hear him*)

BILLY I've been waiting for a chance to tell you *my* news.

ANN (*Offstage*) What is it?

BILLY I've had a break. I'm not going to be at the mercy of my future son-in-law for a handout.

ANN (*Offstage*) You *what?*

BILLY My ex-future son-in-law? My future ex-son-in-law? You know, Eddy. *Anyway.* What I was *trying* to say—I was at this party and ran into Benjamin Wittenberg.

ANN (*Offstage*) Who?

BILLY Benjamin Wittenberg, the big public relations guy. His clients are real biggies—General Motors, AT&T, Raquel Welch, New Zealand . . . Well, we got to talking, and I told him how I'd been feeling lately—you know, about make-up and elevator shoes. Well, he picked it up fast. "You're right, Boylan," he said. He said, "Boylan, I'm not knocking your profession, but when a man reaches forty, he wants to be in the mainstream of American life." So, he sent me up to see a client of his. Federico Orsini.

ANN (*Offstage*) The Italian?

BILLY (*A short take*) What else! The biggest film producer in Italy. He makes dirty Westerns—uses a lot of American people—and they want someone to handle the American and English press. I'd be joining their office in Rome.

ANN (*Entering from the bedroom, dressed in robe and slippers*) Rome? You're going to enter the mainstream of American life by way of Rome?

BILLY (*Hands her a drink*) I thought you'd be pleased for me.

ANN You are abandoning me.

BILLY Who's getting married, you or me?

ANN It's times like this when a person needs friends and support and . . . and affection . . .

BILLY You have young Peter for affection.

ANN It isn't the same thing! You were my husband first!

BILLY Be that as it may, I don't see myself in the role of inseparable friend to the newlyweds. What's eating you, Annie? Still have some doubts about tomorrow?

ANN *No.*

BILLY Then you're okay.

ANN (*Sits down*) It's more complicated than that.

BILLY Ah.

ANN He's . . . he's so touching, Billy . . . the way he tries to make everything easy for me. And he's so damn young. He should be thinking about himself all the time. But he doesn't. He's so considerate and so sensitive to what *I* want—what's right for *me*. (*Pauses*) Who's worrying about what's right for *him*? Oh, Billy, when I stand back and look at him, I can't help seeing how attractive he is. It was a very bad idea to go to the Electric Circus.

BILLY (*Sits wearily on the sofa*) I know what you mean. When you see a whole bunch of them together . . .
    (*He puffs on his cigar*)

ANN He deserves something more than . . .

BILLY Annie, are you absolutely *sure* you're not in love with him?

ANN . . . I love . . . his being in love with me. Would you give me a little more Scotch?

BILLY If you drink any more, you won't sleep.

ANN (*Rises, and goes to the bar*) Why don't we just get smashed. Together. How about it?

BILLY Well, why not? It's my birthday. Thirty-ei . . . Forty-three.

ANN (*Goes to him*) Today's the twenty-second! I'm sorry, darling!

BILLY Don't be sorry. I thought you were displaying the most exquisite politesse. I've stopped looking forward to these little milestones.

ANN Oh, Billy! Thank you for being forty-three. I can't tell you how grateful I am! (*Hugs him*) Happy birthday, darling! (*The doorbell rings*) It's the doorbell.

BILLY Yes, it is. It certainly is.
   (*He puts his cigar in an ashtray*)

ANN Who on earth—?

BILLY (*Gets up*) Christ! It's *Elke!*

ANN Elke?

BILLY I didn't think she'd come down here. She doesn't approve of you.
   (*He goes toward the bedroom*)

ANN Of me! *She* disapproves of *me!* Billy . . . where are you going?

BILLY *(At the bedroom door)* If she finds me here, with *you*, I've had it. Get rid of her. Tell her I was gone when you came home. Act indignant.

ANN I *am* indignant!

BILLY Splendid! Use the Method!
(The doorbell rings again. BILLY *shuts the bedroom door.* ANN *sees the cigar which is smoking in the ash-tray. She grins maliciously, picks the cigar up, puffs vigorously until it's smoking heavily and puts it down in full view, where it cannot be missed. She smiles triumphantly, and then with a seductive sway, goes to the door and opens it.* PETER *stands on the thresh-old.* ANN *catches her breath)*

ANN Oh. You're not Elke! I thought you were . . .

PETER *(Hands her a small bottle)* I was worried you couldn't sleep. I had to go to a couple of guys, but I finally found some.

ANN Oh, Peter, that wasn't necessary . . . I . . .

PETER I thought you'd be in bed . . .

ANN No . . . I mean I haven't . . .

PETER You look all flushed. What's the matter? You don't have a fever, do you?
(Puts out his hand to her forehead. She moves back from him)

ANN No! I'm all right. I'm . . . just surprised to see you . . .
*(*PETER *suddenly is conscious of the cigar smoke. He looks curiously around, spots it, crosses down to coffee table, picks up the cigar, looks at the bedroom door, stubs out the cigar and heads for the front door)*

PETER   I . . . guess I made a mistake . . . coming back un-
expectedly.

ANN   No, no . . .

PETER   Sorry I barged in. I should have known better. Good
night, Ann.
(PETER *closes the door quietly but firmly behind*
him)

ANN   Peter! Wait a minute . . . oh, Peter, let me exp . . .
(*He is gone. She stands frozen, staring at the door.*
After a moment, BILLY *sticks his head out*)

BILLY   All cleared away?

ANN (*Quietly*)   You might say that. (*Suddenly whirls on*
him) Get out of here! Go pollute somebody else's air for a
change! You bastard! You swine! *You goddam actor!*

BILLY (*Astonished at this assault*)   What did I do?

ANN   *Peter!* He saw your cigar and went storming out of
here. (*Starts to cry*) Oh, Billy! I've begged you for years to
give up smoking!

(*She slumps over on the sofa. There is a blackout.*
Then fast gypsy music is heard)

SCENE SIX

The scene is ANN's *apartment. It is late morning, the next day. The curtains are open. Full sunshine streams in.* ANN *paces, and* MRS. MARGOLIN *is seated on an arm of the sofa.*

MRS. MARGOLIN   Two words would clear it all up. You know that.

ANN   Can't you just hear me trying to justify my ex-husband's presence to a twenty . . . (*Takes a deep breath*) to Peter? You should have seen him. Clenched teeth, narrowed eyes! It was too ridiculous—too humiliating.

MRS. MARGOLIN   Humiliation is as humiliation does.

ANN   What does that mean?

MRS. MARGOLIN   I don't know. Call him.

ANN   No. I really don't want to talk to him. I wrote him a letter. Billy took it to him this morning.

MRS. MARGOLIN   Letter? He'll die.

ANN   He's twenty-two. He'll live.

MRS. MARGOLIN   But will you? (*Gets up*) Well, somebody's got to look after the store.

ANN   I'll be there this afternoon.

MRS. MARGOLIN (*Snorts*)   Just what you need. *Call him.*

ANN   Margy, give up. Give up on me.

MRS. MARGOLIN (*At the door*)   Never! Never! There's got to be somebody.
(*BILLY opens the door, and enters*)

BILLY   Hi, Margy.

MRS. MARGOLIN (*Smiles sweetly at Billy. To* ANN)   Anybody but him.
(*She goes*)

BILLY   How is everything?

ANN (*Falsely bright*)   Fine! (*Rises*) How about lunch? Something special. Let's go spend lots of money. You can start getting the feel of the expense-account lunch.

BILLY   Great! Get your coat . . .

ANN   Billy . . . (*She stops*) Now that it's all over . . .

BILLY (*When she doesn't go on*)   What is it, kid?

ANN (*Quietly*)   I've done the right thing, haven't I?

BILLY   You've done the right thing.
(*She starts to go*)

ANN   It was impossible, wasn't it?
(*She stops*)

BILLY   Absolutely. Get your coat.
(ANN *goes into the bedroom.* PETER *comes in the front door. He and* BILLY *look at each other deadpan for a moment.* ANN *reenters with her coat and bag*)

ANN   Let's go to that new—(*Staring at* PETER, *stunned*) Hello, Peter.

PETER (*At the door*)   Hello, Ann.

ANN   How are you?

PETER   I'm all right.

ANN   What are you doing here?

PETER   Our plane leaves in an hour.

ANN   Oh.

PETER   (*Comes down to* ANN)   Look, Ann, I spent the whole night kicking myself, and then I went over to Billy's place and let him kick me . . . and well, here I am. So, say goodbye while I get your bags.
>   (*He puts her coat and bag on a chair, and pushes her toward* BILLY. *He starts for the bedroom*)

ANN   But . . .

BILLY   (*Grabs her shoulders and whispers commandingly*) *Behave.*
>   (PETER *has disappeared into the bedroom*)

ANN   You knew he was coming here.

BILLY   We rode over together.

ANN   Didn't you give him my letter?

BILLY   Letter? Oh, the letter. What the hell did I do with that . . .
>   (*He starts searching his pockets*)

ANN   But, Billy . . .
>   (PETER *comes out with two cases, and sets them down*)

PETER   I'll get the rest of them.
>   (*He starts back for the bedroom*)

ANN   Peter . . .
>   (BILLY *clutches the back of her hair*)

PETER (*Turns back*)   What is it?

ANN   There's . . . I forgot my toothbrush.

PETER (*Goes off*)   I'll get it.

ANN (*Calling after him*)   And my Blush-On. Don't forget my Blush-On.

PETER (*Offstage*)   Blush-On?

ANN   It's in the . . .

BILLY   Second drawer on the left.

ANN (*Turns to* BILLY)   *Why*, Billy? You were so against it.

BILLY (*Shrugs*)   Do you know how many "B" pictures I've made?
    (*They embrace*)

ANN   It's a gigantic mistake.

BILLY (*Solemnly*)   It has been obvious to me for some time that that is what God put us here for. To make gigantic mistakes. It is His Supreme Design.
    (PETER *reenters with two more bags*)

PETER (*Goes to her*)   Is this all?

ANN   I think so.

PETER (*Shakes* BILLY's *hand*)   Thanks, Billy.

BILLY   Beat it.

PETER (*Starting off*)   I'll ring for the elevator (*Pointing to the bags on the floor*) and come back for those two.

BILLY   I'll get them.
    (PETER *goes.* BILLY *gets* ANN's *coat, puts it on her. He takes out the letter from his pocket, and slowly tears it into small pieces and puts them into* ANN's *hand*)

ANN (*Softly*)   Thanks, Billy.

BILLY   I finally decided that you're grown-up enough to marry the kid.

ANN (*Close to tears*)   Goodbye, Billy. (*He emrbaces her; suddenly lets her go, and picks up the bags*) Billy . . .
(*She steps toward* BILLY. PETER *reappears in the doorway*)

PETER   The elevator's here. Come on, love.
(*Greek music begins to play softly*)

BILLY   Go on, hold it. I got these. (PETER *disappears.* BILLY *goes for the bags, and starts for the door*) Come on, Ann.
(ANN *is just standing there.* BILLY, *at the door, stops and looks at her*)

ANN   Oh, dear. . .

BILLY   What's the matter?

ANN   I was just wondering how Helen of Troy managed about her ex-husband.

BILLY   He was an older guy, you know. They let him take care of the luggage.
(*He goes.* ANN, *left alone, looks around the room, walks toward the door, and then looks down at the torn letter in her hand, and flips the pieces into the air as though they were rice or confetti. She flips them so they come down around her head*)

ANN   Here comes the bride. (*Suddenly terrified*) Oh, God!
(*She goes. The music swells*)

Curtain

ABOUT THE AUTHORS

JAY PRESSON ALLEN was born and raised in West Texas, far from Miss Jean Brodie's Edinburgh and the Marcia Blaine School.

She moved to New York and wrote for several of television's dramatic shows, notably the *Philco Playhouse* under the production auspices of Fred Coe.

In 1955 she abandoned writing for several years for marriage and family. Muriel Spark's novel, *The Prime of Miss Jean Brodie,* however, lured her back to writing; she adapted it for producer Robert Whitehead.

Mrs. Allen has written the screenplay for *The Prime of Miss Jean Brodie,* as well as three other screenplays—two for Alfred Hitchcock, and an adaptation of Mary Norton's children's classic *The Borrowers.* David Merrick has also scheduled for fall production Mrs. Allen's *HRH Queen Victoria,* a musical done in collaboration with Charles Strouse and Lee Adams.

Mrs. Allen is married to film and theatre producer Lewis Allen, has an eleven-year-old daughter, Brooke, and lives in New York City and Roxbury, Connecticut.

PIERRE BARILLET and JEAN-PIERRE GREDY, authors of the original comedy *Quarante Carats (Forty Carats),* have been the foremost comedy writing team of the French theatre for the past ten years. Their first play, *Le Don d'Adèle,* ran for three years, followed by the equally successful *Ami, Ami.* Each theatrical season has seen either another original play or an adaptation by the Messrs. Barillet and Gredy. They have adapted several American comedies, among them *Sunday in New York* and *Goodbye Charlie,* which ran concurrently with their great success *Fleur de Cactus,* known here as *Cactus Flower.* Their current success—and one of their biggest hits—now playing in Paris is *4 Pièces sur Jardin.*